Ulrich Schl

Tropical Freshwater
Aquarium
Fish from A to Z

➤ Popular Fish for Freshwater Aquariums
➤ Includes Shrimp, Crabs and Crayfish, and Snails

BARRON'S

Contents

Fish Families

Fish Profiles

Biotope Aquariums

Appendix

Fish Families

Today there are countless numbers of fish species that are kept in aquariums. In the following chapter, you will learn about the characteristics of the individual species and the families to which they belong.

Freshwater Stingrays
Potamotrygonidae

General: About 30 species live in tropical South America in large rivers. Freshwater stingrays from other families are found on other continents as well, but they rarely are imported and do not contain a great many species. All species but one reach a length of at least 2 ft (60 cm) and can be kept only in huge tanks.

Biology: The freshwater stingrays of South America are live-bearing and give birth to fully developed young stingrays after a lengthy gestation period.

Specifics: All the species have a dangerous spine at the end of a whiplike tail, with which they can seriously wound their enemies. Never put your bare hands into a stingray tank, as you may receive a painful wound!

Bichirs
Polypteridae

General: The approximately 12 species live in small and large bodies of water in Africa.

Biology: Bichirs provide no parental care. The young, like newts, possess external gills protruding from the back of the skull, which later disappear.

Specifics: Bichirs can survive in oxygen-poor and hot swamps because they can breathe atmospheric air when the water no longer contains sufficient oxygen. This ability may be the principal reason for their survival as "living fossils" since the age of the saurians in Africa.

Bonytongues
Osteoglossiformes

General: The bonytongues include several fish families that are quite ancient in geological terms: the true bonytongues (Osteoglossidae), the knifefish or

This large ornate bichir smells food.

TIP

Elephant Noses—"Bats" Underwater
They are assigned to the order Osteoglossiformes. By generating a weak electrical field, elephant noses can "communicate" with each other and also explore their surroundings at night or in cloudy or turbulent water—just as bats can locate objects with ultrasound. By the way, the world's largest freshwater fish, *Arapaima gigas*, is also one of the Osteoglossiformes.

featherbacks (Notopteridae), the butterflyfish (Pantodontidae), and the elephant noses or mormyrids (Mormyridae). With the exception of the elephant noses with their 200-odd species, these families contain few species (see TIP, above).

Distribution: Butterflyfish and elephant noses are exclusively native to Africa; knifefish live in Africa and Asia. The true bonytongues occur on all continents.

Biology: Some bonytongue species provide parental care; butterflyfish and many elephant noses pay no attention at all to their offspring. In the latter cases, juveniles must fend for themselves if they are to survive into adulthood.

Knifefish and Electric Eels

Gymnotiformes

General: With the exception of a single Central American species, the more than 100 species, which belong to the families Eigenmanniidae, Apteronotidae, and others, are found in South America.
Biology: Most species are specialized predators of insect larvae and occur in widely varying biotopes. Almost no Gymnotiformes practice parental care.

> **Male black ghost knifefish reach a length of 20 in (50 cm).**

Specifics: Like the elephant noses, electric eels and some knifefish have electric organs that generate discharges used for communication with one another and for orientation.

Catfish

Siluriformes

General: The catfish, with more than 2,000 species, are a species-rich order, repre-

A baby royal pleco (*Panaque nigrolineatus*).

sented by numerous families on every continent (see TIP, below). Of particular significance for aquarium hobbyists are the South American suckermouth armored catfish or plecos (Loricariidae), and the callichthyid armored catfish (Callichthyidae). Of the African species, the naked catfish or squeakers (Mochokidae), are especially popular. Besides these families, many species of which are represented in aquariums, the following enjoy great popularity among hobbyists: sea catfish (Ariidae), long-whiskered or antenna catfish (Pimelodidae), banjo catfish (Aspredinidae), thorny catfish (Doradidae), true catfish (Siluridae), glass catfish (Schilbeidae), frog-mouthed or squarehead catfish (Chacidae), and giant catfish (Pangasiidae).

Biology: Most species are bottom dwelling. Because they are ecologically very diverse, catfish use practically all habitats and all types of food. The males of many species—such as most suckermouth armored catfish—practice parental care, while other species completely

TIP

Catfish—Often Ideal for a Community Tank
The catfish include both the funniest aquarium inhabitants, the callichthyid armored catfish, and some of the most bizarre, such as *Sturisoma festivum*. Catfish are often ideal companions for open-water dwellers, because they inhabit shelters and niches in the substrate not occupied by other aquarium residents. In combination with cichlids, problems may arise if the cichlids extend their territorial claims to the entire tank.

ignore the eggs once they are laid.

Cichlids

Cichlidae

General: With more than 2,000 species, the family Cichlidae is the biggest freshwater fish family. It is widely distributed in South America and Africa, and a very few species are found in Asia. The East African lakes Malawi, Tanganyika, and Victoria alone each have several hundred endemic species.

Biology: All the species have highly developed parental-care patterns. In some species, both parents care for the young, while in others, only one parent participates in the rearing of juvenile cichlids.

TIP

Family Life
Cichlids display intriguing behavioral patterns that make them popular objects of study. It is amazing, for example, that these "simple" fish can construct a complex social system. For example, some Lake Tanganyikan cichlids form virtual extended families, in which the older siblings help raise the younger ones.

Further distinctions are based on how and where the eggs and larvae are tended: Mouthbrooding cichlids take eggs and/or larvae into their mouths and brood them there for several weeks; substrate brooders, on the other hand, lay eggs on a suitable surface (open-water brooders) or in a shelter or cavity (cavity brooders) (see TIP, above).

Gobies

Gobiodei

General: There are approximately 2,000 goby species, most of which are bottom dwellers in seas. They inhab-

Demon earth eaters take their fry back into their mouths if danger threatens.

> The peacock goby guards her clutch of eggs, which adhere to a rock.

it all seas, as well as fresh and brackish waters worldwide. The gobies of importance to aquarium hobbyists belong to the families Gobiidae (true gobies) and Eleotridae (sleeper gobies).
Biology: Most species live near the bottom and feed on various small animals. At spawning time the males occupy territories. They provide parental care for the eggs, which are laid by the female in a sheltered spot. Once the eggs hatch, the males provide no further parental care.

TIP

Gobies—A Private Tip for Hobbyists
Gobies tend to play a subordinate role in the aquarium hobby, although their large number of species and their interesting behaviors merit more attention. If several males of the same species are kept in a fairly large tank, you often can observe efforts to impress, as well as fighting. To prevent serious injuries, make sure your aquarium is well equipped with hiding places.

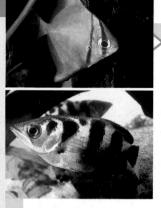

Archerfish often are quite hard to classify.

Fingerfish

Monodactylidae

General: The fewer than 10 species of this perchlike family live in oceans or in brackish water, only rarely in freshwater habitats. They are widely distributed in tropical ocean waters.

Biology: Fingerfish live in groups and are predatory. They do not receive any care from their parents.

Archerfish

Toxotidae

General: The members of this perchlike family are specialized inhabitants of brackish tropical waters. Only a few species live permanently in freshwater habitats.

Biology: Archerfish hunt small fish and insects above and below the water surface. They are well known for their ability to shoot down, with a well-aimed jet of water, insects located on a plant stalk above the water surface, for example. They do not practice parental care; young Archerfish must fend for themselves if they are to survive into adulthood. Many young Archerfish do not reach maturity as a result.

TIP

"Feces Eaters"
The scientific name of the scats, Scatophagus, means "feces eater" and refers to the occurrence of these fish in heavily polluted waters. Nevertheless, in aquariums scats are not as insensitive as their name would suggest. Their needs (brackish water!) must be carefully taken into account, as with all other fish species.

> **Leaf fish mimic dead leaves to perfection.**

Scats

Scatophagidae

General: The few species of this perchlike family inhabit brackish waters in tropical parts of the ocean.
Biology: The sociable scats release buoyant eggs into the water and provide no parental care. They live in groups.

Nandids

Nandidae

General: The few species of this geologically ancient perchlike family live in South America, Africa, and Asia.
Biology: Some species, including the leaf fish, practice parental care: The males devotedly care for the eggs that have been laid and for the hatching larvae until they are free-swimming. All the species are predators of other fish. Their leaflike camouflage allows them to sneak up on their prey and suck it into their protractile mouths all at once.

This male glassfish has changed color as part of his mating ritual.

Tigerperches

Coiidae

General: The four species, which live in brackish water and in rivers of India, Southeast Asia, and New Guinea, are very popular aquarium fish in Asia.

Biology: With their striped pattern, they are extremely well camouflaged in the branches of fallen trees. As far as is known, they do not practice parental care; young Tigerperches are left on their own to survive into adulthood.

Glassfish

Ambassidae

General: Some of the few dozen species do not possess the fascinating glasslike appearance. Except at spawning time, most species live in schools in brackish water or in freshwater habitats along the coasts of tropical seas. At spawning time the males change color and occupy spawning territories. No parental care.

The rainbow snakehead is one of the species that never get very large.

Badids

Badidae

General: This small, perch-like family from southern Asia wins admirers with its splendid colors during mating season.

Biology: The males of some species occupy small caves as their territory and spawn there with several females. Then they guard the eggs and continue to care for the larvae until the young are free-swimming. Once the juveniles are capable of swimming, no further parental care is given.

Snakeheads

Channidae

General: The several dozen species live both in swamps and in small bodies of flowing water in Africa and Asia. Recently, at least one species has been found in North American waters, most likely as a result of careless release.

Biology: They can breathe atmospheric air with a special breathing organ known as the labyrinth (see TIP, below).

TIP

Snakeheads Are Responsible Parents

Some snakehead species orally incubate their eggs for a long while, with both males and females participating in this mouthbrooding process. The fry are fed by the parents with nutrient eggs expelled by the females especially for this purpose. This probably is a consequence of the lack of sufficient food for the young in their biotope. The parents, however, manage better because they can eat insect larvae and small fish.

Labyrinthfish

Anabantoidei

General: The members of this African and Asian fish group, with its more than 100 species, are aquarium highlights. The anabantids include various families. Paradise fish, giant gouramis, and bettas or fighting fish belong to the family Osphronemidae. The kissing gourami is the only species in its family (Helostomatidae; see photo, below). Finally, the bushfish belong to the family of the climbing perches (Anabantidae). See also TIP, right.

See also TIP, right.

TIP

At Home in Various Biotopes
The labyrinthfish species (fighting fish, paradise fish), whose males build foam nests at the water surface, occur mainly in calm waters with an abundance of plants. Other species (some fighting fish and the chocolate gourami) are indigenous to flowing water and are mouthbrooders. Kissing gouramis and large bushfish provide no parental care.

Characins

Characiformes

General: The approximately 1,500 characin species are divided into various families, most of which occur in South America, with a smaller number found in Africa (see TIP, page 17). The characins include these families: moonfish (Citharinidae), hatchetfish (Gasteropelecidae), African tetras (Alestiidae), headstanders (Anostomidae), Hemiodontidae, characins, and tetras (Characidae), and Lebiasinidae.

Kissing gouramis eat only very fine food.

Cypriniforms

Cypriniformes

General: The 2,000-odd species are distributed worldwide, with the excep-

tions of South America and Australia. Cypriniforms, or carp-fish types, are divided into outwardly very diverse families that have little in common apart from their common ancestry. While the free-swimming barbs, danios, and rasboras belong to the family Cyprinidae, most bottom-dwelling species are

> **Pencilfish draw close together when there is a disturbance.**

placed in a group of various loachlike families: river loaches (Balitoridae), loaches (Cobitidae), and algae eaters (Gyrinocheilidae). The Chinese sucker belongs to the family Catostomidae (suckers). Except for the

TIP

The Habits of Characins
Most characiform species are small schooling fish that occur in a wide variety of water types and consume small food organisms. In addition, there are a number of dietary specialists. With few exceptions (piranhas, black darter tetras), characins do not practice parental care. They are very compatible with dwarf cichlids, catfish, and other characins. Most species should be kept as a small group (approximately six specimens).

danios and rasboras, most Cypriniforms of importance in the hobby are bottom-oriented in their search for food and have a diet of plant and animal bottom organisms. Danios and rasboras, however, catch small crustaceans and insects in open water. Most species live gregariously or in a school and do not provide parental care. A few species establish territories that they defend against competitors.

Atheriniforms

Atheriniformes

General: Atheriniforms, which include silversides and rainbowfish, are found in coastal waters worldwide. In some regions, such as Australia and Madagascar, separate families that are true freshwater fish have developed. Among the Atheriniforms important to hobbyists are these families:

Bedotiidae (Madagascar rainbowfish), Melanotaeniidae (rainbowfish), Telmatherinidae (sailfin silversides or Celebes rainbowfish), and Pseudomugilidae (blue-eyes).

Biology: Almost all the species are schooling fish that consume small aquatic animals and live in streams and lakes. The males may become territorial during mating season for short periods. No parental care.

Halfbeaks

Hemiramphidae

General: The halfbeak species of importance to aquarium hobbyists (some 150 species in all) almost always live near the surface in streams, coastal waters, and lakes in Southeast Asia. There they consume insects that fall onto the water surface. Occasionally the males become very aggressive with each other. Most species are live-bearing and give birth to a small number of young.

Rainbowfish display their most splendid colors in the morning sunshine.

TIP

Toothcarps—Perfect "Survival Artists"
Female live-bearing toothcarps are inseminated by the males'
specially modified anal fin (gonopodium). The eggs of many
egg-laying cyprinodonts can survive buried in the riverbed
mud when the waters of their habitat dry up completely.
The parents themselves perish, however. The fry hatch out
with the onset of the next rainy season.

Cyprinodonts

Cyprinodontiformes

General: The cyprinodonts, or toothcarps, include many highly popular aquarium fish. This large group, with more than 1,000 species, is represented on all continents except Australia. Without exception, these are species that never grow very large. They are classified into highly diverse families. The best-known egg-laying cyprinodonts are the killifish of the family Aplocheilidae (old world) and Rivulidae (new world). They include the old-world rivulines (subfamily Aplochelinae) and new-world rivulines (subfamily Rivulinae). Some also assign the (egg-laying)

Dwarf soles, or hogchokers, require a sandy substrate.

If danger threatens, puffers can blow themselves up with water.

Priapella intermedia to the killifish, though they belong in the family Poeciliidae, along with the live-bearing toothcarp. The splitfins (Goodeidae) of Central America, which are also live-bearing, constitute a separate family (see TIP, above).

American Soles

Achiridae

General: Along with soles (Solea solea), the American sole family belongs to the flatfish group, most species of which occur in oceans worldwide and in brackish water (see TIP, right). There are only a few freshwater fish, which are rarely encountered in the aquarium hobby.

Puffers

Tetraodontidae

General: Puffers are found in almost all oceans worldwide. On all tropical continents except Australia, some species have become true freshwater fish.

Biology: Most species are highly specialized predators of snails or fish, which they can crush with their beaklike teeth. Some species provide parental care.

> **TIP**
>
> **Well Camouflaged**
> Most dwarf soles are little predators that hunt insect larvae or young fish. Like all other flatfish, over the course of their evolution they turned "on their side." One side of the body is pale and eyeless, while the other has two eyes. American soles live near sand or mud bottoms and are extremely well disguised. They do not provide parental care.

Pipefish

Syngnathidae

General: Freshwater pipefish belong to the family Syngnathidae (more than 100 species).

Biology: Freshwater pipefish are found worldwide in streams and rivers near coasts, where they consume small aquatic animals and young fish. The females' eggs are deposited in the males' special brooding pouches and hatched out there. Juveniles must then fend for themselves.

> **Spot-finned spiny eels are inquisitive fish that need hiding places.**

Spiny Eels

Mastacembelidae

General: The spiny eels, found in Asia and Africa (about 100 species), are bottom-dwelling predators of insect larvae or fish.

Biology: Most spiny eels are active at night and like to dig themselves into the substrate. Some species even create real subterranean tube homes. At least one species provides parental care.

Fish Profiles

The 300 most popular ornamental fish
species for freshwater aquariums are
arranged here alphabetically, according
to their English common names. The
species are individually profiled, with
information on their characteristics,
the kind of care they require, and tips
on compatibility.

Explanation of the Profiles

English name: The English common name most frequently used.

Latin name: Every animal species that has been scientifically described has a Latin, or scientific, name that appears in *italics*. It has two parts: The first, the generic name, gives the genus and is capitalized; the second, the specific name, is the name of the species and is lowercased.

Also: Additional English vernacular names or an incorrect Latin name that is often erroneously used.

Characteristics: The length of adult animals in inches (in) and centimeters (cm) and pointers for identifying outwardly discernible sexual differences in adult and sexually active animals.

Tank/Water:

➤ Tank: Minimum tank size (length × width × height) for adult animals in inches (in) and centimeters (cm). If you buy young fish, a smaller tank often is adequate. Nevertheless, when buying juveniles, make sure you keep in mind the size they should reach as adults. This holds true despite the repeated claims of some hobbyists that the final size of the fish adapts to the tank size. Admittedly, that sometimes is the case, but it is the result of poor living conditions!

➤ Water type: For every species, we tell you which of seven chemical "water types" is the right range for proper maintenance of the species. The various water types result from the carbonate hardness (in °dH) and the acidity (pH value) of the water. Specialized books on aquariums will provide information on the significance, measurement, and adjustment of the water values.

The seven types are as follows:

Water type 1: pH 4.5–6.5, °dH 0–3

Water type 2: pH 5.5–6.8, °dH 3–8

Water type 3: pH 6.8–7.5, °dH 3–8

Water type 4: pH 6.8–7.5, °dH 8–16

Water type 5: pH 7.2–8.5, °dH > 12

Water type 6: pH 8.0–9.5, °dH 0–3

Water type 7: pH > 8, °dH > 12, with 2 to 3 tablespoons of sea salt per 2.5 gal (10 L) of water.

Care: Data on appropriate living conditions in the

With a length of 5 in (12 cm), the barbatus is the largest of its genus.

aquarium and on the temperament and compatibility of the fish species, as well as tips on tank furnishings and feeding.

Habits: Information on the natural biotope, distribution, diet, and behavior of the species.

Compatibility: Examples of other species with which the fish in question can be successfully combined. If you are interested in keeping it with species not mentioned here, look for a good match in terms of temperament and required living conditions.

Similar species: Advice on species that are closely related and need similar care, with information on length when full grown, which may indicate that you need a different-sized tank to provide appropriate conditions.

Colored grip marks: The gallon (liter) amounts (gal, L) are approximations based on the tank-size information. (One gallon is the equivalent of 4 liters.) The symbol ➤ indicates that the species needs special living conditions.

Adonis Pleco *Acanthicus adonis*

Family: Suckermouth armored catfish or plecos, Loricariidae (see page 9).

Characteristics: 40 in (100 cm). The splendid coloration of the juveniles is replaced by pale spotting in adulthood.

Tank/Water: 128 × 28 × 24 in (320 × 70 × 60 cm), water types 2–5, 76–85°F (24–29°C).

325 gal

Care: Only in very large tanks with lots of roots. A 128-in (320-cm) long tank is adequate for a pair. Feed green foods and high-fiber pellets.

Habits: Found among forest trees that have fallen into the water of large clearwater rivers in the Amazon.

Compatibility: Peaceful species that can be kept with large cichlids and large characins.

African Banded Barb *Barbus fasciolatus*

Also: Blue-barred barb, *Barbus barilioides*

Family: Carp and minnows, Cyprinidae (see page 16).

Characteristics: 2 in (5 cm), female plumper.

Tank/Water: 32 × 14 × 16 in (80 × 35 × 40 cm), water types 2–5, 72–79°F (22–26°C).

25 gal

Care: Keep as a school in dark tanks, densely planted in spots, with low water movement. A soft substrate in parts allows the barbs to dig without injuring their sensitive whiskers.

Habits: Schooling fish from shady streams of the savannah region of southern Africa (Zambia, Angola).

Compatibility: With small to medium-sized African fish, such as upside-down catfish, butterflyfish, or elephant nose.

African Butterfly Cichlid *Anomalochromis thomasi*

Also: *Pelmatochromis thomasi*

Family: Cichlids, Cichlidae (see page 10).

Characteristics: 3 in (8 cm), female somewhat smaller.

Tank/Water: 32 × 14 × 16 in (80 × 35 × 40 cm), water types 2–4, 76–83°F (24–28°C).

25 gal

Care: Calm, reserved species for moderately bright aquariums with dense plantings in parts. Feed all standard foods. Keep in pairs in smaller aquariums.

Habits: Common species in smallish, usually clear rain forest and savannah streams of Liberia and Sierra Leone. Pair-forming open spawner.

Compatibility: With West African tetras (such as *Brycinus longipinnis*) and killifish (*Epiplatys*).

African Butterflyfish *Pantodon buchholzi*

Family: Butterflyfish, Pantodontidae (see page 7).

Characteristics: 5 in (12 cm), male has concave anal fin.

Tank/Water: 40 × 16 × 16 in (100 × 40 × 40 cm), water types 2–5, 81–86°F (27–30°C).

Care: Singly or in groups in aquariums with at least 4 in (10 cm) between the water surface and the tank cover. Water level at least 4 in (10 cm). Feed insects (house crickets, flies, etc.), small fish, and black mosquito larvae. Dry food is rejected or reluctantly accepted. Some floating plants.

Habits: Surface fish indigenous to slow-running streams in West and Central African rain forests and swamps.

Compatibility: With Central African species of the lower tank regions, such as naked catfish.

37.5 gal

African Dwarf Humphead *Steatocranus cf. ubanguiensis*

Family: Cichlids, Cichlidae (see page 10).

Characteristics: 2.75 in (7 cm), males grow larger, develop a larger hump on the head, and have a broader mouth.

Tank/Water: 24 × 12 × 12 in (60 × 30 × 30 cm), water types 3–6, 76–83°F (24–28°C).

Care: Keep in pairs in tanks with good water movement, fine gravelly substrate, and rock caves as hiding places. Accepts high-fiber dry foods and small crustaceans.

Habits: Probably native to rapids of the Kasai, a southern tributary of the Congo. Pair-forming cavity brooder; as an exception, the males pay more attention to the eggs.

Compatibility: With African tetras, in large tanks also with other cichlids (*Teleogramma*).

12.5 gal

African Freshwater Pipefish *Enneacampus ansorgii*

Family: Pipefish, Syngnathidae (see page 21).

Characteristics: 5.5 in (14 cm), male more colorful, with ridge-shaped abdominal brooding pouch.

Tank/Water: 24 × 12 × 12 in (60 × 30 × 30 cm), water types 5–7, 76–83°F (24–28°C).

Care: Keep in larger groups in aquariums with dense vegetation in parts. Feed only live food animals (*Artemia, Cyclops,* white mosquito larvae).

Habits: Native to clear streams, with lots of plants or hiding places, in the coastal region of Central and West Africa. Eats insect larvae and other small animals.

Compatibility: Under no circumstances keep with other fish, because they would get too little food.

12.5 gal

African Knifefish *Xenomystus nigri*
Family: Knifefish, Notopteridae (see page 8).
Characteristics: 9 in (23 cm), female has plumper abdomen.
Tank/Water: $64 \times 24 \times 24$ in ($160 \times 60 \times 60$ cm), water types
2–5, 79–85°F (26–29°C).
Care: Keep singly or in groups (at least five specimens) in
dark, large tanks with many hiding places under roots or in
bamboo canes. Feed these nocturnal fish highly nutritious live
and frozen foods (insects, insect larvae, shrimp), as well as
food tablets.
Habits: Nocturnal predators of insects and shrimp occurring
in various habitats in West and Central Africa.
Compatibility: With larger West African fish: bichirs, butterflyfish, characins. Small fish will be eaten.

125 gal

African Moon Tetra *Bathyaethiops caudomaculatus*
Also: *Bathyaethiops greeni, B. breuseghemi*
Family: African tetras, Alestiidae (see page 16).
Characteristics: About 2 in (5 cm), male larger-finned.
Tank/Water: $32 \times 14 \times 16$ in ($80 \times 35 \times 40$ cm), water types
2–4, 76–81°F (24–27°C).
Care: Group (about 10 fish) for tanks that are not too bright
and have some water movement and loose plantings along the
sides. Takes all smaller foods.
Habits: Schooling fish found in open water in the clearwater
streams of the Congo basin. Not in black water.
Compatibility: For example, with Central African dwarf cichlids (such as *Nanochromis sp.*).
Similar species: *B. altus*, 3 in (8 cm).

37.5 gal

African Red-eyed Characin *Arnoldichthys spilopterus*
Also: African red-eyed tetra, big-scaled African characin
Family: African tetras, Alestiidae (see page 16).
Characteristics: 3 in (8 cm), male has more colorful anal fin.
Tank/Water: $8 \times 16 \times 20$ in ($120 \times 40 \times 50$ cm), water types
2–4, 76–83°F (24–28°C).
Care: Keep at least six specimens in tanks with plenty of open
swimming space, otherwise sparsely furnished. Water move-
ment. Omnivore (prefers mosquito larvae, insects).
Habits: Lively schooling fish found in open water in streams
and small rivers of the Niger Delta in Nigeria.
Compatibility: West African cichlids (such as *Pelvicachromis*
species), naked catfish (*Synodontis* species), swallowtail glass
catfish (*Pareutropius* species).

62.5 gal

Agassiz's Dwarf Cichlid *Apistogramma agassizii*

Family: Cichlids, Cichlidae (see page 10).
Characteristics: 4 in (10 cm), male larger and more colorful.
Tank/Water: 40 × 16 × 16 in (100 × 40 × 40 cm), water types 2–3, 79–83°F (26–28°C).
Care: Dark tanks, densely planted in parts, with several small rock or clay caves. Keep one male with several females.

37.5 gal

Habits: Slow-flowing or standing water in the lowland rain forest of the Amazon. Lives there over the layer of leaf litter. Harem-forming cavity brooder. Takes smaller foods, especially small crustaceans.
Compatibility: With characins that live near the surface or in the middle zone of the tank and an open-brooding dwarf cichlid species, such as *Laetacara sp.*

Akure Aphyosemion *Fundulopanchax gardneri*

Also: *Aphyosemion gardneri*
Family: Killifish, Aplocheilidae (see page 19).
Characteristics: 2.75 in (7 cm), male more colorful and larger.
Tank/Water: 24 × 12 × 12 in (60 × 30 × 30 cm), water types 2–4, 74–81°F (23–27°C).
Care: Keep one male with several females in small, dark tanks.

12.5 gal

Small roots and plant groups provide hiding places when several males are kept together in larger tanks.
Habits: Insect eater that inhabits extremely shallow bank regions of tiny rain forest and savannah streams in Cameroon and Nigeria. Males defend territories.
Compatibility: *Epiplatys,* African barbs (such as *Barbus barilioides*), lampeyes.

Altum Angelfish *Pterophyllum altum*

Also: Deep angelfish, *altum scalare*
Family: Cichlids, Cichlidae (see page 10).
Characteristics: About 6 in (15 cm) long, but up to 13 in (33 cm) high. Can be sexed only with great difficulty.
Tank/Water: 40 × 24 × 32 in (100 × 60 × 80 cm), water types 1–2, 81–86°F (27–30°C).

125 gal

Care: In loosely planted, dark tanks as a group. Include roots that protrude into the tank from above and offer places to hide. Feed a variety of frozen foods and mosquito larvae.
Habits: Peaceful blackwater fish native to Amazonia. Pair-forming open spawner from biotopes with lots of roots.
Compatibility: Dwarf cichlids, armored catfish, *Ancistrus,* larger characins. Neons will be eaten!

Angelfish *Pterophyllum scalare*

Family: Cichlids, Cichlidae (see page 10).

Characteristics: Length up to 6 in (15 cm), height up to 10 in (25 cm). Hard to sex.

Tank/Water: 40 × 20 × 20 in (100 × 50 × 50 cm), water types 2–4, 77–85°F (25–29°C).

Care: Keep as a group in loosely planted tanks, furnished with large-leaved plants and roots that protrude into the tank from above. Feed various frozen foods, mosquito larvae, and dry foods of high nutritive value.

Habits: Peaceful group fish found in larger, usually clear bodies of water in Amazonia. "Stands" quietly among roots and plants. Pair-forming open spawner.

Compatibility: Larger characins (no neon tetras), catfish.

62.5 gal

Angelic Catfish *Synodontis angelicus*

Family: Naked catfish, Mochokidae (see page 9).

Characteristics: About 12 in (30 cm). Final size sometimes given as 22 in (55 cm). Hard to sex.

Tank/Water: 100 × 24 × 24 in (250 × 60 × 60 cm), water types 2–5, 76–83°F (24–28°C).

Care: One or several; each specimen needs its own hiding place. Large tanks with roots. Some can be quarrelsome with another fish, especially if you keep only two specimens. Omnivore.

Habits: Nocturnal species that hides during the day in cracks and caves in submerged dead wood in the current of large rivers of the Congo basin.

Compatibility: Good in display tanks with large African cichlids (such as *Tilapia*) or characins (*Distichodus*).

225 gal

Angelic Pim *Pimelodus pictus*

Family: Long-whiskered or antenna catfish, Pimelodidae (see page 9).

Characteristics: 5 in (12 cm), no known sex differences.

Tank/Water: 64 × 24 × 24 in (160 × 60 × 60 cm), water types 2–5, 77–83°F (25–28°C).

Care: Large tanks with plenty of free swimming space, few shelters, and good water movement, to comply with their need to move around. Omnivore.

Habits: Active swimmers native to larger rivers in the Peruvian Amazon region. They are on the move all day, searching for food.

Compatibility: With all fish that are not too small and are not bothered by their restlessness, such as *Metynnis* or *Myleus*. Fish that are too small might be viewed as food.

125 gal

Armored Bichir *Polypterus delhezi*
Family: Bichirs, Polypteridae (see page 6).
Characteristics: 14 in (35 cm), male has larger anal fin.
Tank/Water: $60 \times 20 \times 20$ in ($150 \times 50 \times 50$ cm), water types 2–6, 79–85°F (26–29°C).
Care: Often aggressive among themselves, better kept singly in aquariums with a hiding place (root, bamboo cane). Feed highly nutritious foods, such as fish meat, shrimp, pellets.
Habits: Nocturnal bottom-dwelling predator from swampy river and lake regions of the Congo basin.
Compatibility: With larger fish from the Congo basin that are not regarded as food: *Distichodus, Synodontis angelicus,* and *Synodontis decorus.*

37.5 gal

Asian Bonytongue *Scleropages formosus*
Also: Asian arowana, dragon fish
Family: True bonytongues, Osteoglossidae (see page 6).
Characteristics: 35 in (90 cm), hard to sex.
Tank/Water: $157 \times 59 \times 32$ in ($400 \times 150 \times 80$ cm), water types 2–5, 81–85°F (27–29°C).
Care: Keep singly or in groups in very large aquariums with some roots along the sides. Feed highly nutritious foods including shrimp, fish, and insects.
Habits: Predator that hunts prey at the surface of slow-flowing and standing waters in Southeast Asia.
Compatibility: Keep only with large, peaceful fish such as giant catfish, Siamese tigerfish, or large barbs.
Caution: Protected species! Covered by CITES.

1250 g

Astatotilapia latifasciata
Also: *Haplochromis sp. "Zebra obliquidens"*
Family: Cichlids, Cichlidae (see page 10).
Characteristics: 5.25 in (13 cm), male larger and bright in color.
Tank/Water: $48 \times 20 \times 20$ in ($120 \times 50 \times 50$ cm), water types 4–6, 76–81°F (24–27°C).
Care: Keep one or many males together with several females in well-lit tanks with large-leaved plants and some rocks. Feed all standard foods, especially food containing small crustaceans.
Habits: Known to be native only to Lake Nawampasa in Uganda. Considered "threatened" in the wild. Not pair-forming; maternal mouthbrooder.
Compatibility: With cichlid species from Lake Victoria, such as *Paralabidochromis* and *Pundamilia* species.

75 gal

Bala Shark *Balantiocheilos melanopterus*
Also: Silver shark, *Balantiocheilus melanopterus*
Family: Carp and minnows, Cyprinidae (see page 16).
Characteristics: 14 in (35 cm), male slimmer.
Tank/Water: 100 × 24 × 24 in (250 × 60 × 60 cm), water types
2–5, 76–83°F (24–28°C).

225 gal

Care: Group fish only for very large aquariums. Plenty of open
swimming space and few structures along the tank sides. Feed
highly nutritious dry food containing plant matter, as well as
small crustaceans as a frozen food. Keeping them in small
tanks is animal cruelty!
Habits: Agile large barb from rivers and lakes of Southeast
Asia. Considered a threatened species in its native habitat.
Compatibility: With other larger fish of Southeast Asia.

Banded Rainbowfish *Melanotaenia trifasciata*
Family: Rainbowfish, Melanotaeniidae (see page 18).
Characteristics: 4.3–6 in (11–15 cm) (varies by population),
male more colorful.
Tank/Water: 64 × 24 × 24 in (160 × 60 × 60 cm), water types
4–6, 76–83°F (24–28°C).

150 gal

Care: Schooling fish for large tanks with loose plantings along
the sides and lots of open swimming space. Small to medium-
sized live and dry foods (such as water fleas).
Habits: The populations, which vary in appearance, are native
to rain forest and savannah rivers in Australia.
Compatibility: Good with all fish that are not overly small and
have similar water requirements, also with Lake Tanganyikan
cichlids, for example.

Banjo Catfish *Bunocephalus coracoideus*
Also: Bunocephalus bicolor
Family: Banjo catfish, Aspredinidae (see page 9).
Characteristics: 5 in (12 cm), female plumper.
Tank/Water: 24 × 12 × 12 in (60 × 30 × 30 cm), water types
2–5, 77–83°F (25–28°C).

12.5 gal

Care: Relatively small tanks are adequate for these relatively
inactive fish. Sand or leaves important as substrate, since they
enjoy burrowing there. Feed worms and small live foods.
Habits: Leaf layer or sand in calm waters of the Amazon system. They molt periodically.
Compatibility: Only with medium-sized fish of the mid-
regions of the tank; small ones may be eaten.
Similar species: *Bunocephalus knerii*, 6 in (15 cm).

Barbatus *Scleromystax barbatus*
Family: Callichthyid armored catfish, Callichthyidae (see page 9).
Characteristics: 5 in (12 cm), female more compact and plumper.
Tank/Water: 48 × 20 × 20 in (120 × 50 × 50 cm), water types 3–5, 72–79°F (22–26°C).

75 gal

Care: Needs areas with soft substrate, some shelters in the form of plants, roots, or rocks, and plenty of open swimming space as well. Feed all small to medium-sized foods, also dry foods. Use special food as for *Corydoras*.
Habits: Gregarious fish found in soft-bottomed areas of medium-sized rivers in eastern South America.
Compatibility: Ideal companion for South American fish of the middle and upper tank strata.

Beacon Fish *Hemigrammus ocellifer*
Also: Head- and taillight fish
Family: Tetras, Characidae (see page 16).
Characteristics: 2 in (5 cm), female plumper and less colorful.
Tank/Water: 32 × 14 × 16 in (80 × 35 × 40 cm), water types 2–5, 76–83°F (24–28°C).

25 gal

Care: As a school of at least eight specimens in dark tanks, densely planted in parts. Fine dry and frozen foods.
Habits: Very common schooling fish found mainly in slow-flowing and standing waters in Amazonia and Guyana. The reflecting spot on the caudal fin base is visible even in dark waters and may play a role in keeping the school together.
Compatibility: Unproblematic companion for all smaller and medium-sized South American fish, such as angelfish.

Black Calvus *Altolamprologus calvus*
Family: Cichlids, Cichlidae (see page 10).
Characteristics: 5.5 in (14 cm), females are much smaller.
Tank/Water: 40 × 20 × 20 in (100 × 50 × 50 cm), water types 5–6, 77–81°F (25–27°C).

62.5 gal

Care: Singly or in pairs in rocky tanks with at least one cave (for example, large sea snail shells) into which the female fits but the male does not. Feed live and frozen foods (small crustaceans), no dry foods.
Habits: Predator of shrimp and small fish, found in rocky areas of Lake Tanganyika where there are many crevices in the rocks. A loner. Pair-forming cavity brooder.
Compatibility: This species particularly recommended as a tankmate for larger Lake Tanganyikan cichlids.

Black Darter Tetra *Poecilocharax weitzmani*

Also: Black morpho tetra

Family: Tetras, Characidae (see page 16).

Characteristics: 2 in (5 cm), male larger-finned and more colorful.

Tank/Water: 24 × 12 × 12 in (60 × 30 × 30 cm), water types 1–3, 79–85°F (26–29°C).

2.5 gal

Care: Keep two males with several females in an aquarium with narrow tube-shaped hiding places. Demanding where water quality is concerned. These fish accept only live food.

Habits: Unlike "normal" tetras, this fish inhabits small caves and lives in hiding; the males are territorial and even perform brood care. Origin: drainage area of the Rio Negro.

Compatibility: Only with peaceful surface dwellers.

Black Ghost Knifefish *Apteronotus albifrons*

Family: Knifefish, Apteronotidae (see page 8).

Characteristics: 20 in (50 cm), female has a shorter snout.

Tank/Water: 100 × 24 × 24 in (250 × 60 × 60 cm), water types 2–5, 76–83°F (24–28°C).

225 gal

Care: Keep one male with up to five females in a tank with roots and tubes as hiding places for each specimen. Accepts frozen and live foods (mosquito larvae, tubifex).

Habits: Nocturnal species found in Amazonia, in many sandy-bottomed flowing waters. Communicates and finds its way by emitting weak electric signals. Eats insect larvae.

Compatibility: With larger peaceful fish from South America, such as angelfish, discus, and catfish.

Similar species: *Apteronotus leptorhyncus,* 10.6 in (27 cm).

Black Molly *Poecilia sphenops var.*

Family: Live-bearing toothcarp, Poeciliidae (see page 20).

Characteristics: 3–5 in (8–12 cm), male has a copulatory organ.

Tank/Water: 32 × 14 × 16 in (80 × 35 × 40 cm), water types 5–6, 79–85°F (26–29°C).

25 gal

Care: Warmth-loving fish that should be kept in groups in densely planted aquariums with plenty of swimming space. Feed primarily plant matter, as well as dry food. Sometimes susceptible to disease; adding salt often helps (water type 7).

Habits: The original form is from a group of fish found in fresh and brackish waters in Central America.

Compatibility: Good companion fish, but only if the proper water values (temperature, type) are maintained.

Black Neon Tetra *Hyphessobrycon herbertaxelrodi*

Family: Tetras, Characidae (see page 16).
Characteristics: 1.5 in (4 cm), female plumper.
Tank/Water: 24 × 12 × 12 in (60 × 30 × 30 cm), water types 2–4, 76–83°F (24–28°C).
Care: Popular species thanks to its robustness; best kept in dark, densely planted aquariums. Feed smaller foods, also dry food. Keep at least eight specimens.
Habits: Schooling fish of the middle tank region, native to various waters of the Mato Grosso (Brazil).
Compatibility: With tetras, callichthyid armored catfish, suckermouth armored catfish, and dwarf cichlids.
Similar species: Purple tetra, *Hyphessobrycon metae,* 1.5 in (4 cm), *Hyphessobrycon loretoensis,* 1.5 in (4 cm).

12.5 gal

Black Phantom Tetra *Hyphessobrycon megalopterus*

Also: *Megalomphodus megalopterus*
Family: Tetras, Characidae (see page 16).
Characteristics: 1.75 in (4.5 cm), male has longer fins.
Tank/Water: 24 × 12 × 12 in (60 × 30 × 30 cm), water types 2–5, 74–79°F (23–26°C).
Care: A few males and several females in dark tanks with dense plantings along the sides and small solitary plants. All smaller foods.
Habits: Group fish native to shady and plant-rich waters in southern Brazil. Males are territorial.
Compatibility: With South American dwarf cichlids (such as *Apistogramma* species) or small callichthyid armored catfish and surface fish (such as Lebiasinidae).

12.5 gal

Black Ruby Barb *Puntius nigrofasciatus*

Family: Carp and minnows, Cyprinidae (see page 16).
Characteristics: 2.75 in (7 cm), female paler.
Tank/Water: 40 × 16 × 16 in (100 × 40 × 40 cm), water types 2–5, 70–76°F (21–24°C).
Care: The splendid coloring of the males is brought out only in dark tanks with loose plantings, such as *Cryptocoryne.* Sandy substrate in parts will allow the barbs to burrow for all food types, especially plant foods.
Habits: Gregarious, lively inhabitant of clear and cool rain forest streams in Sri Lanka, where it eats chiefly algae over gravel or sand bottoms.
Compatibility: Loaches (*Schistura*), as well as rasboras and danios.

37.5 gal

Black Widow Tetra *Gymnocorymbus ternetzi*
Family: Tetras, Characidae (see page 16).
Characteristics: 2.4 in (6 cm), male smaller and slimmer. The shiny black coloration becomes less intense with increasing age and is replaced by dark gray.
Tank/Water: 32 × 14 × 16 in (80 × 35 × 40 cm), water types 2–6, 74–83°F (23–28°C).

25 gal

Care: Keep this undemanding, peaceful species in groups (at least six to eight specimens) in loosely planted community tanks that are not too brightly lit. Accepts all small foods.
Habits: Schooling fish native to shady, quiet flowing waters of the Rio Paraguay system in southern Brazil.
Compatibility: Best with hardy dwarf cichlids, callichthyid armored catfish, and other tetras.

Black-banded Leporinus *Leporinus fasciatus*
Family: Headstanders, Anostomidae (see page 16).
Characteristics: 12 in (30 cm), hard to sex.
Tank/Water: 100 × 24 × 24 in (250 × 60 × 60 cm), water types 2–5, 76–83°F (24–28°C).

250 gal

Care: As a group (at least five specimens) in large unplanted aquariums furnished with plenty of roots to add structure. Individuals often aggressive. Feed green foods and frozen animal foods.
Habits: Agile swimmer found in fast-flowing waters in rocky stretches in Amazonia, where it forages for plant and animal foods.
Compatibility: With large South American fish such as silver dollars, large cichlids, and catfish.

Black-bellied Limia *Limia melanogaster*
Also: Blue limia
Family: Live-bearing toothcarp of the family Poeciliidae (see page 20).
Characteristics: 2.5 in (6.5 cm), male has copulatory organ.
Tank/Water: 24 × 12 × 12 in (60 × 30 × 30 cm), water types 4–6, 72–83°F (22–28°C).

12.5 gal

Care: Moderately lit aquariums with both loosely and densely planted parts and with gentle water movement; two or three males with six or more females. Feed flakes containing plant matter, and small live and frozen foods.
Habits: Lively inhabitant of streams. Surface fish.
Compatibility: Small Central American cichlids (*Archocentrus*) or blind cave characins.

Bleeding Heart Tetra *Hyphessobrycon erythrostigma*

Family: Tetras, Characidae (see page 16).

Characteristics: 3 in (8 cm), male slimmer, with more elongated finnage.

Tank/Water: 40 × 20 × 20 in (100 × 50 × 50 cm), water types 2–4, 76–83°F (24–28°C).

62.5 gal

Care: This splendid species is most effective as a school in dark tanks with large-leaved plants (*Echinodorus*) and some room to swim. Takes all standard foods; small crustaceans (*Cyclops*, *Artemia*) intensify the red coloration.

Habits: Found in blackwater streams of the upper Amazon in Brazil. Eats insects (larvae) and small crustaceans.

Compatibility: Ideal with classical blackwater fish, such as altum angelfish or *Apistogramma*.

Bleher's Rainbowfish *Chilatherina bleheri*

Family: Rainbowfish, Melanotaeniidae (see page 18).

Characteristics: 5.5 in (14 cm), male more colorful, many color variants among males.

Tank/Water: 60 × 20 × 20 in (150 × 50 × 50 cm), water types 4–6, 77–83°F (25–28°C).

87.5 gal

Care: Bright, ideally sunny tanks with loose plantings along the sides and plenty of open swimming space. Feed all smallish to medium-sized foods.

Habits: Schooling fish from the plant-rich shore areas of Lake Bira in New Guinea. Males display the most beautiful colors in the morning hours.

Compatibility: Larger gobies, but also barbs, characins, peaceful cichlids, and catfish.

Bloodfin Tetra *Aphyocharax anisitsi*

Family: Tetras, family Characidae (see page 16).

Characteristics: 2.2 in (5.5 cm), male slimmer and more colorful.

Tank/Water: 32 × 14 × 16 in (80 × 35 × 40 cm), water types 2–5, 72–81°F (22–27°C).

25 gal

Care: Keep as a small school in aquariums that are densely planted in parts. Feed all standard foods.

Habits: Paraná River system in southern South America. Probably native to flowing, plant-rich streams.

Compatibility: Low-maintenance species for a South American community aquarium, for example, with armored catfish (*Corydoras*) or dwarf cichlids (*Apistogramma*), bristlenosed catfish (*Ancistrus*), and *Hyphessobrycon* tetras.

Blue Acara *"Aequidens" cf. pulcher*
Also: *"Aequidens" latifrons*
Family: Cichlids, Cichlidae (see page 10).
Characteristics: 6 in (16 cm), female somewhat smaller.
Tank/Water: 48 × 20 × 20 in (120 × 50 × 50 cm), water types 2–5, 76–83°F (24–28°C).

75 gal

Care: If kept in pairs, it is undemanding, needing only a few shelters and a varied diet of all standard foods.
Habits: Rivers, ditches, and flood areas in northern South America. Pair-forming open spawner.
Compatibility: Suckermouth armored catfish and larger characins.
Similar species: There are various blue acara species, which are very similar.

Blue Emperor Tetra *Inpaichthys kerri*
Family: Characins, Characidae (see page 16).
Characteristics: 1.75 in (4.5 cm), female smaller and paler.
Tank/Water: 24 × 12 × 12 in (60 × 30 × 30 cm), water types 2–4, 74–79°F (23–26°C).

12.5 gal

Care: A group of a few males and several females in tanks that are not too harshly lit, with loose plantings. Takes all smaller foods.
Habits: Group fish, thus far found only in streams in the Aripuana River system in Brazil. The males temporarily form and defend mating territories against other males.
Compatibility: With other small characins, small suckermouth armored catfish, and callichthyid armored catfish. In larger tanks, also with dwarf cichlids.

Blue Gourami *Trichogaster trichopterus*
Family: Osphronemidae (see page 16).
Characteristics: 5 in (12 cm), female smaller with rounded fins.
Tank/Water: 40 × 16 × 16 in (100 × 40 × 40 cm), water types 2–6, 72–81°F (22–27°C).

37.5 gal

Care: In aquariums furnished with plenty of structures: floating plants, loose plantings along the sides, and roots. Feed high-quality flaked foods (green flakes), various live and frozen foods. Place only one pair in 3.5-ft (1-m) tanks.
Habits: Usually found in standing, often cloudy, waters in Indonesia and Malaysia. Often occurs in rice fields as well.
Compatibility: With Asian bottom fish (loaches, catfish) and calm barbs, danios, and rasboras.
Similar species: Various cultivated forms, all about 5 in (12 cm).

Blue Gularis *Fundulopanchax sjoestedti*
Also: *Aphyosemion sjoestedti*
Family: Killifish of the family Aplocheilidae (see page 19).
Characteristics: 3.5–5.5 in (9–14 cm), male far more colorful.
Tank/Water: 32 × 12 × 12 in (80 × 30 × 30 cm), water types 2–4, 74–81°F (23–27°C).

25 gal

Care: One male with several females in dark tanks, densely planted in parts. Use roots to provide retreats for the often hotly courted females. Feed highly nutritious live food.
Habits: Native to swampy water bodies that partially dry up during the dry season in West Cameroon's coastal lowlands. Only the eggs survive in the dried-out bottom until the next rainy season ("seasonal fish").
Compatibility: Not suitable for community tanks.

Blue Neon Cichlid *Paracyprichromis nigripinnis "Neon"*
Family: Cichlids, Cichlidae (see page 10).
Characteristics: 4 in (10 cm), male has more intense colors.
Tank/Water: 40 × 20 × 20 in (100 × 50 × 50 cm), water types 5–6, 77–81°F (25–27°C).

62.5 g

Care: As a group in tanks that have at least one dark part (created, for example, by an overhanging rock structure); otherwise, the species will remain pale. Varied diet of frozen and live small crustacean foods.
Habits: Lives free-swimming near dark, rocky areas of Lake Tanganyika.
Compatibility: Do not keep with the more aggressive *Cyprichromis* species.
Similar species: *Paracyprichromis brieni,* 4 in (10 cm).

Blue Tetra *Mimagoniates microlepis*
Also: *Coelurichthys microlepis*
Family: Tetras, Characidae (see page 16).
Characteristics: 3.5 in (9 cm), male more intensely colored.
Tank/Water: 40 × 16 × 16 in (100 × 40 × 40 cm), water types 2–5, 76–79°F (24–26°C).

37.5 gal

Care: Schooling fish, loves to swim, likes moderately bright tanks with loose plantings along the sides and good water movement. Feed small insects (fruit flies) and black mosquito larvae, as well as dry foods. Keep two or three males with six or more females.
Habits: Nervous fish found in clear streams of eastern Brazil.
Compatibility: With current-loving South American stream fish, such as panda corys, *Corydoras panda.*

Boeseman's Rainbowfish *Melanotaenia boesemani*

Also: Ajamaru rainbowfish
Family: Rainbowfish, Melanotaeniidae (see page 18).
Characteristics: 5.5 in (14 cm), male more brightly colored.
Tank/Water: 48 × 20 × 20 in (120 × 50 × 50 cm), water types 4–6, 77–83°F (25–28°C).
Care: Schooling fish for large, brightly lit tanks with loose plantings along the sides and plenty of open swimming space. Feed all smallish to medium-sized foods.
Habits: Schooling fish from vegetation-rich bank areas of waters in New Guinea's Ajamaru lake district.
Compatibility: Good companion fish for small species.
Similar species: *M. lacustris,* 5 in (12 cm), but keep at 68–77°F (20–25°C).

75 gal

Bolivian Ram *Mikrogeophagus altispinosus*

Also: *Papiliochromis altispinosus*
Family: Cichlids, Cichlidae (see page 10).
Characteristics: 3 in (8 cm), male has longer fins.
Tank/Water: 40 × 16 × 16 in (100 × 40 × 40 cm), water types 2–4, 79–85°F (26–29°C).
Care: Keep in pairs in loosely to densely planted tanks with root-wood structures and some flat stones. Feed all standard foods, especially live foods: small crustaceans, mosquito larvae.
Habits: Quiet shore areas of fairly large bodies of flowing water and streams in northern Bolivia. Pair-forming open spawner.
Compatibility: With South American tetras or cavity-brooding dwarf cichlids such as *Apistogramma.*

37.5 gal

Borelli's Dwarf Cichlid *Apistogramma borellii*

Also: Yellow dwarf cichlid, *Apistogramma reitzigi*
Family: Cichlids, Cichlidae (see page 10).
Characteristics: 2.75 in (7 cm), male larger and more colorful.
Tank/Water: 24 × 12 × 12 in (60 × 30 × 30 cm), water types 2–4, 72–76°F (22–24°C).
Care: Keep in pairs even in relatively small tanks at least 24 in (60 cm) long, densely planted in parts (with floating plants as well) and equipped with small caves as hiding places. Accepts all smaller foods.
Habits: In Bolivia and neighboring areas, usually found in clear still or slow-flowing waters with many aquatic plants. Usually a pair-forming cavity brooder.
Compatibility: With small characins.

12.5 gal

Brevis Shell Dweller *Neolamprologus brevis*

Family: Cichlids, Cichlidae (see page 10).
Characteristics: 2.4 in (6 cm), female smaller, with yellowish belly.
Tank/Water: 24 × 12 × 12 in (60 × 30 × 30 cm), water types 5–6, 77–81°F (25–27°C).
Care: Some requirements are a sand layer about 2 in (5 cm) deep and a few empty snail shells. Keep in pairs. Feed small crustaceans (*Cyclops, Artemia*), also dry foods.
Habits: Lives in pairs in empty snail shells in Lake Tanganyika. Unlike other snail-dwelling cichlids, this species lives and spawns in pairs and occupies a single snail shell jointly.
Compatibility: In large tanks, with Lake Tanganyikan cichlids that are not sand dwellers (such as *Cyprichromis*).

12.5 gal

Brichard's Slender Cichlid *Teleogramma brichardi*

Family: Cichlids, Cichlidae (see page 10).
Characteristics: 5 in (12 cm), female has broad white band on upper half of caudal fin.
Tank/Water: 48 × 16 × 16 in (120 × 40 × 40 cm), water types 3–5, 76–81°F (24–27°C).
Care: In pairs, with good water movement and lots of hiding places formed by stone slabs lying flat, so that the fish can dig out hollows underneath them. The numerous hiding places are necessary to give harried females a place to retreat.
Habits: Found in rock cracks in the area of the Lower Congo rapids. In spawning season, females have a red belly against a black background. Pair-forming cavity brooder.
Compatibility: Congo tetras and humphead cichlids.

50 gal

Brichard's Synodontis *Synodontis brichardi*

Family: Naked catfish or squeakers, Mochokidae (see page 9).
Characteristics: 6 in (15 cm), hard to sex.
Tank/Water: 60 × 20 × 20 in (150 × 50 × 50 cm), water types 3-4, 76–81°F (24–27°C).
Care: Keep as a group (at least five specimens) in spacious aquariums with water movement and stone slabs as hiding places. Feed a varied diet, including different types of frozen foods and plant-based flake foods. No red mosquito larvae—they cause digestive problems.
Habits: Found in the Lower Congo rapids. The flat body profile and suckerlike mouth are adaptations to the turbulent water conditions of its native habitat.
Compatibility: *Nanochromis parilus* and Congo tetras.

100 gal

Bronze Cory *Corydoras aeneus*

Also: Black aeneus
Family: Callichthyid armored catfish, Callichthyidae (see page 9).
Characteristics: 2.4 in (6 cm), female plumper.
Tank/Water: 24 × 12 × 12 in (60 × 30 × 30 cm), water types 2–6, 77–83°F (25–28°C).

12.5 gal

Care: Keep as a group in tanks with sandy substrate in parts, loose plantings, and structures where the fish can go to rest. Feed fine live, frozen, and dry foods. Use special *Corydoras* food!
Habits: Gregarious inhabitants of soft-bottomed stretches of water throughout South America.
Compatibility: Ideal companion for South American fish of the middle and upper tank regions. In small tanks, do not keep with cichlids.

Brown Pencilfish *Nannostomus eques*

Also: *Nannobrycon eques*
Family: Lebiasinidae (see page 16).
Characteristics: 2 in (5 cm), female plumper.
Tank/Water: 24 × 12 × 12 in (60 × 30 × 30 cm), water types 2–4, 79–85°F (26–29°C).

12.5 gal

Care: Dark tanks with floating and stem plants, thin roots. No water movement. Feed small insects, black mosquito larvae, dry foods.
Habits: Distinctive fish found near the surface of quiet rivers and lakes in the Amazon region, where it apparently eats insects. Slant-swimmer.
Compatibility: As a surface fish, good with demanding small fish of the Amazon that inhabit the lower tank regions.

Buenos Aires Tetra *Hemigrammus caudovittatus*

Family: Tetras, Characidae (see page 16).
Characteristics: 2.75 in (7 cm), female less colorful.
Tank/Water: 40 × 16 × 16 in (100 × 40 × 40 cm), water types 2–6, 68–76°F (20–24°C).

37.5 gal

Care: Robust schooling fish that loves to swim and is content in all aquariums, provided they have enough open swimming space and are planted with robust species. Eats tender shoots of aquatic plants. Feed plant-based dry foods.
Habits: Found in plant-rich marshy pools in the drainage area of the Paraná and Uruguay River systems in South America.
Compatibility: Thanks to its robustness, a good companion fish for many species, even those that like somewhat cooler water, such as *Corydoras paleatus*.

Buffalohead Cichlid *Steatocranus casuarius*

Family: Cichlids, Cichlidae (see page 10).

Characteristics: 5.5 in (14 cm), males grow larger, develop a bigger hump on the head, and have a wider mouth.

Tank/Water: 40 × 16 × 16 in (100 × 40 × 40 cm), water types 3–6, 76–83°F (24–28°C).

37.5 gal

Care: In pairs in tanks with water movement and some caves that the fish can enlarge by digging. Food: high-fiber dry and frozen foods.

Habits: Bottom-dwelling fish of the Lower Congo rapids. Lives chiefly on algae. Pair-forming cavity brooder.

Compatibility: With other open-water fish from the Congo, such as Congo tetras. In large tanks also with other cichlids, such as *Teleogramma brichardi*.

Bulldog Pleco *Chaetostoma spec.*

Family: Suckermouth armored catfish, Loricariidae (see page 9).

Characteristics: About 3–5 in (8–12 cm), male has wider mouth.

Tank/Water: 24 × 12 × 12 in (60 × 30 × 30 cm), water types 3–5, 68–76°F (20–24°C).

12.5 gal

Care: Keep in strongly lit tanks with high water movement. Don't let the water get too warm in summer! Feed green foods as well as dry food tablets.

Habits: *Chaetostoma* are native to cool mountain waters in the Andes, where they rasp algae from pebbles in the strong current at the surface.

Compatibility: Best kept in a species tank.

Similar species: Various species are being introduced, some of them hard to classify.

Bumblebee Goby *Brachygobius cf. doriae*

Also: *Brachygobius xanthozona*

Family: Gobies, Gobiidae (see page 11).

Characteristics: 1.4 in (3.5 cm), female plumper.

Tank/Water: 24 × 12 × 12 in (60 × 30 × 30 cm), water types 5–7, 81–86°F (27–30°C).

12.5 gal

Care: Keep about 12 specimens in a small tank with many (salt-tolerant) plants or small hiding places. Takes fine foods exclusively. No dry foods.

Habits: Native to weed-filled sections of rivers near coasts and brackish-water areas of Southeast Asia, often made clear and dark tea-colored by humic substances.

Compatibility: Best kept by themselves, as they would quickly starve if forced to compete for food.

Bushnose Catfish *Ancistrus sp.*
Family: Suckermouth armored catfish, Loricariidae (see page 9).
Characteristics: 5.5 in (14 cm), male has "antennas" on his head.
Tank/Water: 32 × 14 × 16 in (80 × 35 × 40 cm), water types 2–6, 76–85°F (24–29°C).

25 gal

Care: Keep in pairs in tanks with wood roots to rasp at and roots or clay caves as retreats. Feed vegetable foods and dry foods. Algae eater.
Habits: Peaceful eater of algae and young growth; also constantly rasps away at wood as a source of fiber. Exact origin and classification of this fish, the most popular algae eater in the hobby, still unknown.
Compatibility: Ideal companion for almost all aquarium fish with the possible exception of small dwarf cichlids.

Butterfly Splitfin *Ameca splendens*
Also: Butterfly goodeid
Family: Goodeid topminnows, Goodeidae (see page 20).
Characteristics: 5 in (12 cm), male has yellow-bordered tail.
Tank/Water: 48 × 16 × 16 in (120 × 40 × 40 cm), water types 4–6, 70–76°F (21–24°C).

50 gal

Care: Peaceful group fish for tanks with plenty of water movement, bright lighting, and lots of space to swim. Loosely planted along the sides with robust plants. Feed plant matter, as well as live, frozen, and dry foods.
Habits: Clear flowing waters with rocky sections and lush plant growth in the highlands of Mexico.
Compatibility: Ideal companion fish for small and medium-sized Central American cichlids.

Cape Lopez Lyretail *Aphyosemion australe*
Family: Killifish, Aplocheilidae (see page 19).
Characteristics: 2.4 in (6 cm), male larger and more colorful.
Tank/Water: 24 × 12 × 12 in (60 × 30 × 30 cm), water types 2–4, 70–76°F (21–24°C).

12.5 gal

Care: In a 24-in (60-cm) tank, keep about three males with six to eight females. Dark tank, planted in parts, furnished with small, fine roots as a place of retreat. Feed small insects and other small live foods. No dry food.
Habits: Insect eater found in shallow, shady streams of Gabon's coastal lowlands, in the rain forest.
Compatibility: With small African barbs (such as *Barbus barilioides*) or lampeyes.
Similar species: *Aphyosemion ahli*, 2.4 in (6 cm).

Cardinal Tetra *Paracheirodon axelrodi*

Family: Tetras, Characidae (see page 16).
Characteristics: Up to about 1.5 in (4 cm), female plumper.
Tank/Water: $24 \times 12 \times 12$ in ($60 \times 30 \times 30$ cm), water types 1–4, 74–81°F (23–27°C).
Care: Keep as a school in dark tanks, which can be loosely planted. No harsh lighting. Feed all small foods.

12.5 gal

Habits: Common, gregarious group fish native to the clear waters of flooded forests in the drainage area of the Rio Negro and the Orinoco (South America).
Compatibility: With dwarf cichlids (*Apistogramma*), callichthyid armored catfish (*Corydoras*), and surface-dwelling characins, such as *Carnegiella strigata*. Not with angelfish, which can easily consume a cardinal tetra.

Celebes Halfbeak *Nomorhamphus liemi*

Family: Halfbeaks, Hemirhamphidae (see page 18).
Characteristics: 3.5 in (9 cm), male more brightly colored.
Tank/Water: $40 \times 16 \times 16$ in ($100 \times 40 \times 40$ cm), water types 3–5, 68–76°F (20–24°C).
Care: Elongated tanks with plenty of water movement and furnished with pebbles and hiding places. Plantings along the sides in tanks with low water movement. One male with several females. Highly nutritious live foods (young house crickets, fry of other fish species). Dry food as supplement.

625 gal

Habits: Group fish that hunts insects in hill streams on the Indonesian island of Sulawesi.
Compatibility: With hillstream fish from other geographic regions, such as *Gastromyzon* or *Chaetostoma*.

Celebes Rainbowfish *Marosatherina ladigesi*

Also: *Telmatherina ladigesi*
Family: Celebes rainbowfish, Telmatherinidae (see page 18).
Characteristics: 2.75 in (7 cm), male longer-finned.
Tank/Water: $40 \times 16 \times 16$ in ($100 \times 40 \times 40$ cm), water types 4–6, 77–83°F (25–28°C).
Care: Fish for bright tanks with loose plantings and lots of open swimming space. Small live foods, also dry foods. Sensitive to poor water maintenance.

37.5 gal

Habits: Lively schooling fish indigenous to lime-rich streams in a single karst area on the island of Sulawesi (Celebes).
Compatibility: With all fish that live near the bottom and tolerate relatively limy water, for example, also with cichlids from Lake Tanganyika, such as *Julidochromis* species.

Checkerboard Cichlid *Dicrossus filamentosus*

Family: Cichlids, Cichlidae (see page 10).
Characteristics: 3.5 in (9 cm), male has long-tipped fins.
Tank/Water: $40 \times 16 \times 16$ in ($100 \times 40 \times 40$ cm), water types 1–2, 81–86°F (27–30°C).

37.5 gal

Care: In tanks densely planted in parts, but with open swimming space above sand or fine gravel areas. Keep one male with two or three females. Feed fine live, frozen, and dry foods.
Habits: Found in shallow clear water and black water in the Rio Negro catchment basin (Amazonia). Harem-forming open spawner.
Compatibility: Also in the wild with cardinal tetra.
Similar species: *Dicrossus maculatus*, 4 in (10 cm) (water types 2–4).

Checkered Barb *Puntius oligolepis*

Family: Carp and minnows, Cyprinidae (see page 16).
Characteristics: About 2 in (5 cm), male more intensely colored, with black-bordered dorsal and anal fin.
Tank/Water: $24 \times 12 \times 12$ in ($60 \times 30 \times 30$ cm), water types 2–6, 74–81°F (23–27°C).

12.5 gal

Care: Keep a few males, several females in loosely planted, bright tanks with soft substrate and some pebbles. All small foods.
Habits: Bottom-dwelling group fish from clearwater streams and marshy pools in upland regions of Sumatra (Indonesia). Males establish mating territories.
Compatibility: Good with the genus *Danio*, loaches of the genus *Schistura*, but also with platys and swordtails.

Cherry Barb *Puntius titteya*

Family: Carp and minnows, Cyprinidae (see page 16).
Characteristics: 2 in (5 cm), male more intensely colored.
Tank/Water: $24 \times 12 \times 12$ in ($60 \times 30 \times 30$ cm), water types 2–4, 74–81°F (23–27°C).

12.5 gal

Care: Keep a few males with several females in dark tanks loosely planted with *Cryptocoryne* species. Soft substrate. Varied diet of small live, frozen, and dry foods.
Habits: Placid, middle-water-dwelling species found in dark, slow-flowing streams in Sri Lanka's virgin forests. Males are territorial during mating period, with "glowing" colors.
Compatibility: Only with peaceful fish that inhabit the middle and upper water strata, such as labyrinthfish of the genus *Colisa* or *Pseudosphromenus*.

Chinese Algae Eater *Gyrinocheilus aymonieri*

Family: Algae eaters, Gyrinocheilidae (see page 17).
Characteristics: 10 in (25 cm), males stay smaller.
Tank/Water: $80 \times 20 \times 20$ in ($200 \times 50 \times 50$ cm), water types 2–6, 76–83°F (24–28°C).

125 gal

Care: Large, strongly lit tanks with strong water movement. Large pebbles and shelters in the form of stone slabs to provide retreats. Feed plants (such as lettuce leaves, cucumber slices) and "green" dry foods. Keep as a group (at least six) or singly.
Habits: Algae eater that rasps algae from pebbles in fast-flowing stretches of streams in Thailand. A few old specimens are aggressive at times.
Compatibility: With nimble Asian barbs (such as *Puntius fasciatus*) or rasboras and danios (such as *Devario* species).

Chinese Sailfin Sucker *Myxocyprinus asiaticus*

Family: Suckers, Catostomidae (see page 17).
Characteristics: 24 in (60 cm), hard to sex. Young much more brightly colored than low-contrast old fish.
Tank/Water: $138 \times 32 \times 32$ in ($350 \times 80 \times 80$ cm), water types 3–6, 61–81°F (16–27°C).

37.5 gal

Care: Only in very large tanks with strong filtration and several roots under which the fish can rest. Feed pellets containing vegetable matter. The 138-in (350-cm) length given here is suitable in the long term only for fish that are not fully grown. Don't let the juveniles' cute appearance lead you to make a bad buy!
Habits: The species is native to the Yangtse River in China. It has high edible value and is bred in ponds.
Compatibility: Other Asian "giant fish."

Chocolate Gourami *Sphaerichthys osphromenoides*

Family: Gouramis, Osphronemidae (see page 16).
Characteristics: 2 in (5 cm), male has light-edged anal fin.
Tank/Water: $40 \times 16 \times 16$ in ($100 \times 40 \times 40$ cm), water type 1, 76–81°F (24–27°C).

37.5 gal

Care: Keep about six specimens in blackwater conditions: mineral-poor water with peat filtration, substrate made of sterilized peat (change regularly). Power filter to provide water movement. Roots as hiding and resting places. Feed small live foods, including *Drosophila.*
Habits: Current-loving group fish native to Southeast Asian blackwater canals. Hunts insect larvae. Males may be aggressive toward each other.
Compatibility: With other blackwater fish of the region.

Clown Killi *Epiplatys annulatus*

Also: *Pseudepiplatys annulatus*

Family: Killifish, Aplocheilidae (see page 19).

Characteristics: 1.75 in (4.5 cm), male has more colorful caudal fin.

Tank/Water: 24 × 12 × 12 in (60 × 30 × 30 cm), water types 2–4, 79–83°F (26–28°C).

12.5 gal

Care: Keep one male with several females in densely planted tanks with cover of floating plants. Feed dry food and fine live foods.

Habits: Insect-eating surface fish found in clear and plant-rich swampy waters in West Africa.

Compatibility: Good companion fish for small African fish of the lower and middle tank regions, such as dwarf cichlids (*Pelvicachromis*), *Neolebias ansorgii*, or *Barbus fasciolatus*.

Clown Knifefish *Chitala ornate*

Also: Spotted featherback, *Notopterus chitala*

Family: Knifefish or featherbacks, Notopteridae (see page 7).

Characteristics: 40 in (100 cm), no sexual differences known.

Tank/Water: 120 × 32 × 32 in (320 × 80 × 80 cm) for juveniles, otherwise only for display aquariums, water types 2–6, 76–83°F (24–28°C).

500 gal

Care: Predatory fish, must be kept singly or as a group in enormous aquariums. Provide large shelters. When buying, don't be enticed by the juveniles' beautiful coloration. Feed high-nutrient foods, such as trout pellets and fish meat.

Habits: Nocturnal fish found in the rivers of Southeast Asia.

Compatibility: With other large Asian fish, such as green arowana, Siamese tigerfish, or giant barbs.

Clown Loach *Botia macracanthus*

Family: Loaches, Cobitidae (see page 17).

Characteristics: 10 in (25 cm), hard to sex. Be careful when catching them: small spine under each eye!

Tank/Water: 100 × 24 × 20 in (250 × 60 × 50 cm), water types 1-5, 77–86°F (25–30°C).

187.5 gal

Care: Group fish (keep at least five specimens); each one needs its own shelter, for example, in a bamboo cane. Some specimens are often quarrelsome. Spacious tanks with sandy substrate in parts and with roots.

Habits: Found in rivers on the islands of Sumatra and Borneo. Despite its popularity, little is known about its habits.

Compatibility: With warmth-loving larger Asian barbs, gouramis, and catfish.

Cochu's Blue Tetra *Boehlkea fredcochui*

Family: Tetras, Characidae (see page 16).
Characteristics: About 2 in (5 cm), female plumper.
Tank/Water: 32 × 14 × 16 in (80 × 35 × 40 cm), water types 2–5, 74–79°F (23–26°C).
Care: Keep a school of about 10 specimens in tanks not too harshly lit, furnished with a dark substrate and loose plantings, with strong water movement. Feed all smaller foods.
Habits: Schooling fish, fond of swimming, native to clear streams of the Amazon (Peru).
Compatibility: With all small to mid-sized fish species that are not bothered by their hectic behavior, such as *Corydoras* and suckermouth armored catfish, as well as robust dwarf cichlids (such as *Apistogramma*).

25 gal

Cockatoo Dwarf Cichlid *Apistogramma cacatuoides*

Family: Cichlids, Cichlidae (see page 10).
Characteristics: 3.5 in (9 cm), male larger and more colorful.
Tank/Water: 40 × 16 × 16 in (100 × 40 × 40 cm), water types 2–4, 76–79°F (24–26°C).
Care: Planted, dark aquariums with a few caves (such as halves of coconut shells). Keep one male with several females. All standard foods; don't forget foods containing small crustaceans.
Habits: Shallow areas with leaf litter in small flowing water bodies and residual pools of the Peruvian Amazon (clear and white water). Harem-forming cavity brooder.
Compatibility: With South American characins that live near the surface, and with other surface fish.
Similar species: *Apistogramma juruensis*, 3 in (8 cm).

37.5 gal

Colombian Tetra *Hyphessobrycon columbianus*

Also incorrectly: "Hyphessobrycon ecuadoriensis"
Family: Tetras, Characidae (see page 16).
Characteristics: 1.75 in (4.5 cm), female higher-backed and plumper.
Tank/Water: 24 × 12 × 12 in (60 × 30 × 30 cm), water types 3-4, 76–83°F (24–28°C).
Care: Densely planted, dark tanks. Keep at least six to eight specimens. Feed fine live, frozen, or dry foods.
Habits: Found only in a small stream in Colombia's Darién forest. The tetras are found in shallow water, in shady spots with leaf litter.
Compatibility: With other small South American tetras, *Corydoras*, or dwarf cichlids.

12.5 gal

Common Freshwater Goby *Rhinogobius sp.*
Also: White-cheeked goby, *Rhinogobius wui*
Family: Gobies, Gobiidae (see page 11).
Characteristics: 2 in (5 cm), male colorful.
Tank/Water: 24 × 12 × 12 in (60 × 30 × 30 cm), water types 4–6, 65–76°F (18–24°C).
Care: Keep three males with about six females in a 16-gal (60-L) stream aquarium with sand, pebbles, and small caves. Water movement beneficial. Feed fine live and frozen foods; virtually impossible to get it used to dry foods.
Habits: Stream-dwelling species from Southeast Asia. Males form territories around their hiding place.
Compatibility: Rasboras and danios (*Danio* and *Tanichthys*).
Similar species: There are many *Rhinogobius* species.

12.5 gal

Common Hatchetfish *Gasteropelecus sternicla*
Family: Hatchetfish, Gasteropelecidae (see page 16).
Characteristics: 2.4 in (6 cm), male plumper when spawning.
Tank/Water: 40 × 16 × 16 in (100 × 40 × 40 cm), water types 2–5, 77–83°F (25–28°C).
Care: Spacious tanks with gentle water movement at the surface. Some floating plants advantageous. Insect foods (fruit flies, black mosquito larvae), after break-in period, also dry foods. Keep at least six specimens.
Habits: Surface fish found in the streams and swamps of Amazonia. Lives in groups right under the surface and eats mainly small insects. Able to "fly" short distances over water.
Compatibility: With all small to medium-sized fish of the middle and lower tank regions.

37.5 gal

Congo Dwarf Cichlid *Nanochromis parilus*
Also: *Nanochromis nudiceps*
Family: Cichlids, Cichlidae (see page 10).
Characteristics: 2.75 in (7 cm), female has conspicuously colored dorsal fin.
Tank/Water: 32 × 14 × 16 in (80 × 35 × 40 cm), water types 3-4, 76–81°F (24–27°C).
Care: Keep in pairs in aquariums with sand and numerous hiding places for the females. Water movement. Takes all standard foods, especially insect larvae.
Habits: Lives in rapids of the lower Congo, where the species inhabits areas in which the flow is less swift. Eats insect larvae. Pair-forming cavity brooder.
Compatibility: With cichlids of the Congo rapids.

25 gal

Congo Puffer *Tetraodon miurus*
Family: Puffers, Tetraodontidae (see page 20).
Characteristics: 6.3 in (16 cm), hard to sex.
Tank/Water: 48 × 20 × 20 in (120 × 50 × 50 cm), water types 3–6, 79–83°F (24–28°C).
Care: Keep singly in tanks with a deep layer of fine gravel and with water movement. Feed live small food fish; other live foods are only reluctantly accepted.
Habits: Lurking predator that buries itself and waits, with its upward-directed mouth, to feed on fish that swim past in the frequently strong current of the Congo and its tributaries. Often only the keenly watchful eyes of the buried fish are visible.
Compatibility: Only with large fish of the upper tank regions, such as moonfish or large cichlids.

75 gal

Congo Tetra *Phenacogrammus interruptus*
Family: African tetras, Alestiidae (see page 16).
Characteristics: 3.5 in (9 cm), adult male has more intense colors and elongated fins.
Tank/Water: 48 × 20 × 20 in (120 × 50 × 50 cm), water types 2–4, 74–81°F (23–27°C).
Care: Keep at least six specimens in well-lit tanks with open swimming space. Nutritious live and frozen foods (mosquito larvae, insects), also dry food. Water movement.
Habits: Lively schooling fish native to small and large clearwater streams in the Congo basin. Lives mainly on insects that fly near the water surface.
Compatibility: Dwarf cichlids (such as *Nanochromis* or *Teleogramma* species) and naked catfish of the Congo basin.

75 gal

Convict Cichlid *Archocentrus nigrofasciatus*
Also: Marbled convict, zebra cichlid, *Cryptoheros nigrofasciatus, Cichlasoma nigrofasciatum*
Family: Cichlids, Cichlidae (see page 10).
Characteristics: 6 in (15 cm), female smaller and more colorful.
Tank/Water: 40 × 20 × 20 in (100 × 50 × 50 cm), water types 5–6, 74–81°F (23–27°C).
Care: Undemanding species for tanks with fine gravel substrate, lots of structures, and a rock cave. Takes all standard foods.
Habits: Lives in very diverse biotopes in Central America. Pair-forming cavity brooder.
Compatibility: With agile live-bearing toothcarp, such as swordtails (*Xiphophorus helleri*).
Similar species: *Archocentrus septemfasciatus,* 5 in (12 cm).

62.5 gal

Convict Julie *Julidochromis regani*
Also: Regan's julie
Family: Cichlids, Cichlidae (see page 10).
Characteristics: 6 in (15 cm), hard to sex.
Tank/Water: 40 × 16 × 16 in (100 × 40 × 40 cm), water types 5–6, 77–81°F (25–27°C).

37.5 gal

Care: Keep in pairs in tanks furnished with many rocks as hiding places. Feed all standard foods. Over the years the young, as they grow and mature, will produce a large extended family.
Habits: Rocky coastal sections of Lake Tanganyika that include some sandy areas. Eats small invertebrates. Usually a pair-forming cavity brooder.
Compatibility: With Lake Tanganyikan cichlids that do not inhabit the rocky zones, such as *Paracyprichromis*.

Coolie Loach *Pangio kuhlii*
Also: *Pangio semicincta, Acanthophthalmus kuhlii*
Family: Loaches, Cobitidae (see page 17).
Characteristics: About 3 in (8 cm), hard to sex; be careful when catching this fish—it has a spine beneath each eye!
Tank/Water: 24 × 12 × 12 in (60 × 30 × 30 cm), water types 2–5, 76–86°F (24–30°C).

12.5 gal

Care: Gregarious fish. Keep several in densely planted (Java moss), dark (floating-plant cover) tanks. Soft substrate. Feed smaller live, frozen, and dry foods.
Habits: Nocturnal fish that hides during the day. In an aquarium it does come out in the daytime to forage for food. Found in vegetation-rich streams and standing water bodies in Malaysia.
Compatibility: Danios and rasboras (*Boraras, Rasbora*).

Coral Red Pencilfish *Nannostomus mortenthaleri*
Also: *Nannostomus marginatus mortenthaleri*
Family: Lebiasinidae (see page 16).
Characteristics: 2 in (5 cm), female plumper and less colorful.
Tank/Water: 24 × 12 × 12 in (60 × 30 × 30 cm), water types 2–5, 74–79°F (23–26°C).

12.5 gal

Care: Keep a few males with several females in dark tanks loosely planted with stem plants. Takes small live and dry foods.
Habits: Males defend small territories around individual plants. Streams of the Peruvian Amazon.
Compatibility: With bottom dwellers (callichthyid armored catfish) or bottom-oriented characins (*Hemigrammus*, neon tetras). In larger tanks, with dwarf cichlids.
Similar species: Golden pencilfish, *N. beckfordi*, 2.4 in (6 cm).

Cross-dressing Dwarf *Nanochromis transvestitus*

Family: Cichlids, Cichlidae (see page 10).
Characteristics: 2.4 in (6 cm), female has more contrasting coloration—white-striped caudal fin and red belly.
Tank/Water: 24 × 12 × 12 in (60 × 30 × 30 cm), water types 1–2, 77–83°F (25–28°C).
Care: Specialized blackwater fish that becomes sickly in harder and alkaline water. Easy to feed—dry food and various frozen foods.
Habits: As far as is known, the species is endemic to Lake Maj Ndombe, a shallow blackwater lake in the Congo. Eats insect larvae. Pair-forming cavity brooder.
Compatibility: Best with other softwater fish native to the Congo basin, such as Congo tetras.

12.5 gal

Cuckoo Catfish *Synodontis multipunctatus*

Also: Many-spotted catfish
Family: Naked catfish, Mochokidae (see page 9).
Characteristics: 5 in (12 cm), hard to sex.
Tank/Water: 64 × 24 × 24 in (160 × 60 × 60 cm), water types 5–6, 77–81°F (25–27°C).
Care: Spacious aquariums with rock structures that the fish can swim through. Varied diet of frozen and dry foods. Keep at least four or five specimens.
Habits: Gregarious fish from Lake Tanganyika, where it eats snails and other invertebrates. These fish use spawning mouth-brooding cichlids as a host for the eggs.
Compatibility: With mouthbrooding cichlids from Lake Tanganyika, such as *Cyathopharynx, Tropheus*.

150 gal

Cupid Cichlid *Biotodoma cupido*

Family: Cichlids, Cichlidae (see page 10).
Characteristics: 5.25 in (13 cm), females somewhat smaller.
Tank/Water: 32 × 20 × 16 in (80 × 50 × 40 cm), water types 2–5, 77–83°F (25–28°C).
Care: Keep in pairs in small tanks at least 32 in (80 cm) long. It is better to keep a group in larger tanks; then pairs will form. Furnish tank with large-leaved plants, flat stones, and fine gravel substrate. Feed all smaller foods.
Habits: Found in various slow-flowing or standing waters in the Amazon River basin. This pair-forming and open-spawning species commonly occurs in open areas.
Compatibility: In larger tanks with *Apistogramma*, South American characins, *Ancistrus* suckermouth armored catfish.

37.5 gal

Deepwater Haplochromis *Placidochromis electra*
Also: *Haplochromis electra*
Family: Cichlids, cichlidae (see page 10).
Characteristics: 6 in (15 cm), female relatively colorless.
Tank/Water: 64 × 24 × 24 in (160 × 60 × 60 cm), water types 5–6, 77–81°F (25–27°C).

150 gal

Care: As a group (one or many males with several females) in tanks with a 2-in (5-cm) layer of sand and several rocks. Feed all standard foods, especially mix containing crustaceans (shrimp mixes), mosquito larvae, and frozen *Artemia*.
Habits: Inhabits sandy bottoms in Lake Malawi. Maternal mouthbrooder; does not form pairs.
Compatibility: Do not put with rock-dwelling Lake Malawi cichlids, such as *Copadichromis* or *Aulonocara*.

Demason's Cichlid *Pseudotropheus demasoni*
Family: Cichlids, Cichlidae (see page 10).
Characteristics: 3 in (8 cm), male has somewhat stronger colors.
Tank/Water: 40 × 20 × 20 in (100 × 50 × 50 cm), water types 5–6, 77–81°F (25–27°C).

62.5 gal

Care: Keep a group of about 20 specimens in tanks furnished with rock structures arranged so that the fish can swim through them. Aggressions disappear only if kept as a group. Feed plant-based dry food and small crustaceans.
Habits: Algae and plankton eater found in the rock zone of Lake Malawi. Very aggressive with others of its species. Maternal mouthbrooder; does not form pairs.
Compatibility: With Lake Malawi rock cichlids.
Similar species: *Pseudotropheus saulosi*, 3.5 in (9 cm).

Demon Eartheater *Satanoperca cf. leucosticta*
Also: *Satanoperca jurupari, Geophagus jurupari*
Family: Cichlids, Cichlidae (see page 10).
Characteristics: 10 in (25 cm), hard to sex.
Tank/Water: 80 × 24 × 24 in (200 × 60 × 60 cm), water types 2–5, 79–85°F (26–29°C).

175 gal

Care: Keep about six specimens in tanks with sand or fine gravel substrate and roots as shelters. Feed various types of frozen foods, dry food.
Habits: Inhabitant of sandy areas in larger flowing waters of the Amazon. Uses its gills to sift insect larvae out of the sand. Pair-forming open spawner or mouthbrooder.
Compatibility: With peaceful giant cichlids from South America (such as *Heros*), tetras, and catfish.

Desert Goby *Chlamydogobius eremius*

Family: Gobies, Gobiidae (see page 11).
Characteristics: 2.4 in (6 cm), male has colored fins.
Tank/Water: 24 × 12 × 12 in (60 × 30 × 30 cm), water types 4–6, 68–79°F (20–26°C).
Care: Two males with several females. Sandy substrate with rocks for digging caves. Feed small live and frozen foods and dry food containing algae. Turning off the heating at night approximates the natural temperature drop during the night.
Habits: Territorial fish found in Lake Eyre, in the central Australian desert.
Compatibility: Schooling fish of the upper water strata, such as *Marostherina* in fairly large tanks.

12.5 gal

Diamond Tetra *Moenkhausia pittieri*

Family: Tetras, Characidae (see page 16).
Characteristics: 2.4 in (6 cm), male longer-finned and more brightly colored.
Tank/Water: 40 × 20 × 20 in (100 × 50 × 50 cm), water types 2–4, 76–83°F (24–28°C).
Care: Tank with floating-plant cover and dim light. Loose plantings and a few roots complete the furnishings. The beautiful colors develop only in softer water. Feed all standard foods, including dry food.
Habits: Little is known about the habitat near Lake Valencia in Venezuela.
Compatibility: Splendid species for a community tank with demanding species (water values!), such as altum angelfish.

62.5 gal

Discus *Symphysodon aequifasciatus*
Also: Discus fish, *Symphysodon aequifasciata*

Family: Cichlids, Cichlidae (see page 10).
Characteristics: 7 in (18 cm), difficult to sex.
Tank/Water: 40 × 20 × 20 in (100 × 50 × 50 cm), water type 2, 79–86°F (26–30°C).
Care: Keep in groups (six to eight specimens) in loosely planted, dark tanks. Decor should include roots protruding into the tank from above to provide hiding places. Feed dry and frozen foods especially made for discus.
Habits: Peaceful species that lives in groups in biotopes of the Amazon River basin, where roots abound, and eats insect larvae.
Compatibility: With peaceful South American tetras and bottom-dwelling fish (such as *Ancistrus dolichopterus*).

62.5 gal

Dwarf Corydoras *Corydoras hastatus*
Family: Callichthyid armored catfish, Callichthyidae (see page 9).
Characteristics: 1.4 in (3.5 cm), female plumper and bigger.
Tank/Water: 24 × 12 × 12 in (60 × 30 × 30 cm), water types
2–6, 77–83°F (25–28°C).
Care: Tiny schooling fish for densely planted, bright tanks.
Keep at least 6–10 specimens. Feed fine live and frozen foods
(such as *Cyclops* or *Artemia* nauplii), but dry food too.
Habits: One of the few armored catfish that swim in open
water eagerly and often. Lives in weed-filled areas of small
bodies of water in Mato Grosso, Brazil.
Compatibility: Only with small fish, such as bottom-dwelling
callichthyid armored catfish and small characins.
Similar species: Pygmy cory, *Corydoras pygmaeus,* 1.2 in (3 cm).

12.5 gal

Dwarf Croaking Gourami *Trichopsis pumila*
Also: *Trichopsis pumilus*
Family: Gouramis, Osphronemidae (see page 16).
Characteristics: 1.5 in (4 cm), male has pointed dorsal fin.
Tank/Water: 24 × 12 × 12 in (60 × 30 × 30 cm), water types
2–6, 74–81°F (23–27°C).
Care: In pairs or in small groups in densely planted tanks, with
floating plants and shelters under roots. Takes fine live and dry
foods.
Habits: Males form territories and emit clearly audible
"croaks." Inhabits weed-filled ponds or ditches of continental
Southeast Asia.
Compatibility: With other extremely tiny fish, such as excla-
mation-point rasboras, *Boraras urophthalmoides*.

12.5 gal

Dwarf Flag Cichlid *Laetacara curviceps*
Also: *Aequidens curviceps*
Family: Cichlids, Cichlidae (see page 10).
Characteristics: 2.75 in (7 cm), hard to sex.
Tank/Water: 24 × 12 × 12 in (60 × 30 × 30 cm), water types
2–4, 79–86°F (26–30°C).
Care: Keep in pairs in tanks that are densely planted in parts,
with a few lime-free pebbles. Feed primarily fine live foods, but
also dry foods.
Habits: Found along the banks in low-current areas of plant-
rich waters in the Amazon basin. Pair-forming open spawner.
Compatibility: Peaceful species, suitable for community aquariums with calm tetras; in large tanks, with cavity-brooding
dwarf cichlids.

12.5 gal

Dwarf Gourami *Colisa lalia*
Family: Gouramis, Osphronemidae (see page 16).
Characteristics: 2.4 in (6 cm), male larger and more colorful.
Tank/Water: 24 × 12 × 12 in (60 × 30 × 30 cm), water types 2–6, 76–83°F (24–28°C).
Care: Keep in pairs in small tanks; in tanks at least 40 in (100 cm) long, in small groups. Use plenty of structures and plants (floating plants), so that the female has a place to retreat to. Takes all smaller foods.
Habits: Peaceful fish found in swampy and weedy canals, quiet zones of rivers, and flooded areas in India. Eats animal and plant foods.
Compatibility: With small and moderately lively Asian fish of the middle and lower tank regions, such as barbs and rasboras.

12.5 gal

Dwarf Livebearer *Heterandria formosa*
Family: Live-bearing toothcarp, Poeciliidae (see page 20).
Characteristics: 1.4 in (3.5 cm), male has copulatory organ.
Tank/Water: 24 × 12 × 12 in (60 × 30 × 30 cm), water types 4–6, 65–83°F (18–28°C).
Care: Keep as a group in densely planted smaller aquariums. Feed fine live foods (*Artemia*, *Cyclops*), but also dry foods. Somewhat cooler conditions in winter promote vitality.
Habits: Found among plants in small and very tiny bodies of standing water in southeastern North America. Sometimes bothers slow fish by nipping at their fins.
Compatibility: Only with other small fish species that also tolerate cooler water from time to time, such as peppered catfish (*Corydoras paleatus*).

12.5 gal

Dwarf Loach *Botia sidthimunki*
Also: Chain loach
Family: Loaches, Cobitidae (see page 17).
Characteristics: 2.4 in (6 cm), female plumper. Be careful when fishing this species out—there's a small spine under each eye!
Tank/Water: 24 × 12 × 12 in (60 × 30 × 30 cm), water types 2–6, 79–85°F (26–29°C).
Care: In planted tanks with plenty of structures. Small live and dry foods.
Habits: Found in still, often cloudy areas in waters of some rivers and their floodplains, mainly in Thailand and Indochina. A gregarious species that often swims in open water.
Compatibility: Ideal companion fish for smaller Asian fish that inhabit the middle and upper tank strata.

12.5 gal

Dwarf Neon Rainbowfish *Melanotaenia praecox*
Also: Neon rainbowfish
Family: Rainbowfish, Melanotaeniidae (see page 18).
Characteristics: 2.4 in (6 cm), male more intensely colored.
Tank/Water: 32 × 14 × 16 in (80 × 35 × 40 cm), water types 2–5, 74–81°F (23–27°C).

25 gal

Care: Schooling fish for dark tanks with low water movement, gravel bottom, and plants along the sides. Feed live, frozen, and dry foods.
Habits: Stream fish found in the forest streams of New Guinea's Mamberano River system. In the wild, its diet probably consists chiefly of insects, mainly ants, that fall into the water.
Compatibility: With bottom-dwelling stream fish, such as *Gastromyzon* or *Pseudomugil furcatus*.

Dwarf Pencilfish *Nannostomus marginatus*
Family: Pencilfish, Lebiasinidae (see page 16).
Characteristics: 1.4 in (3.5 cm), female plumper and less colorful.
Tank/Water: 24 × 12 × 12 in (60 × 30 × 30 cm), water types 2–3, 74–77°F (23–25°C).

12.5 gal

Care: About two or three males with six females in tanks that are densely planted in parts. Prefers live food (such as *Artemia* nauplii); takes frozen foods and plant-based dry foods.
Habits: Standing-water fish that lives in Amazonia in waters covered with lush vegetation. Pecks at algae and food animals. The males defend small courtship territories.
Compatibility: With small fish of the lower tank region, such as callichthyid armored catfish or dwarf cichlids.

Dwarf Puffer *Carinotetraodon travancoricus*
Family: Puffers, Tetraodontidae (see page 20).
Characteristics: 1.25 in (3 cm), male more intensely colored.
Tank/Water: 24 × 12 × 12 in (60 × 30 × 30 cm), water types 5–7, 72–76°F (22–24°C).

12.5 gal

Care: As a group in loosely planted aquariums with fine gravelly substrate. Highly nutritious diet: exclusively live foods such as white mosquito larvae, snails.
Habits: Active small fish from weed-filled, marshy ponds in India.
Compatibility: Only with nimble schooling fish such as rasboras. Otherwise, especially if food is scarce, the species tends to nip other fishes' fins.
Similar species: *C. imitator*, 1.25 in (3 cm).

Dwarf Rainbowfish *Melanotaenia maccullochi*
Family: Rainbowfish, Melanotaeniidae (see page 18).
Characteristics: 2.75 in (7 cm), male slimmer and more colorful.
Tank/Water: $32 \times 14 \times 16$ in ($80 \times 35 \times 40$ cm), water types 4–6, 76–86°F (24–30°C).
Care: Aquariums that are densely planted in some parts and loosely planted in others, with strong lighting and gentle water movement. Keep at least six to eight specimens. Varied diet of small live, frozen, and dry foods.
Habits: Schooling fish found in swamps and streams with clear, acid water with many aquatic plants.
Compatibility: With all small bottom and surface fish that need the same water conditions.

25 gal

Dwarf Rasbora *Boraras maculata*
Also: Spotted rasbora, *Rasbora maculata*
Family: Carp and minnows, Cyprinidae (see page 16).
Tank/Water: $24 \times 12 \times 12$ in ($60 \times 30 \times 30$ cm), water types 1–3, 77–85°F (25–29°C).
Care: Schooling fish (at least 10–20 specimens) for dark soft-water tanks with peat filtration. Plantings of fine-leafed plants. Feed fine live and sometimes also dry foods.
Habits: Lives in western Malaysia and Sumatra (Indonesia) near banks of slow-flowing or standing waters, in areas with lots of plants or leaf litter.
Compatibility: Only with other dwarf fish, such as small bottom fish like *Pangio kuhlii.*

12.5 gal

Dwarf Scarlet Badis *Dario dario*
Also: *Badis sp. "Scarlet," Badis badis bengalensis*
Family: Badids, Badidae (see page 15).
Characteristics: 1.2 in (3 cm), female paler and plumper.
Tank/Water: $24 \times 12 \times 12$ in ($60 \times 30 \times 30$ cm), water types 2–4, 76–81°F (24–27°C).
Care: In a 15.85 gal (60-L) tank with dense vegetation and some oak leaves that have been soaked in water, you can keep two males with four or five females. Eats fine live and frozen foods; does not accept dry food.
Habits: Native to weed-filled streams in northern India.
Similar species: *Badis badis,* once a frequently kept badid species, 2.4 in (6 cm), is calmer and needs little caves.

12.5 gal

Dwarf Suckermouth *Otocinclus ssp.*

Family: Suckermouth armored catfish, Loricariidae (see page 9).

Tank/Water: $24 \times 12 \times 12$ in ($60 \times 30 \times 30$ cm), water types 2–6, 72–81°F (22–27°C).

Care: Keep at least five or six specimens in well-planted and brightly lit aquariums. Good algae eater! Feed plant-based foods, including food tablets.

Habits: Gregarious species usually found in groups near river banks where vegetation hangs into the water, in Amazonia.

Compatibility: With all small fish whose needs are identical to those of the otos.

Similar species: *Otocinclus vittatus* (lacks spot), 1.5 in (4 cm).

12.5 gal

Electric Blue Haplochromis *Sciaenochromis fryeri*

Also: Electric blue ahli, *Sciaenochromis ahli*

Family: Cichlids, Cichlidae (see page 10).

Characteristics: 8 in (20 cm), male blue, female colorless.

Tank/Water: $64 \times 20 \times 20$ in ($160 \times 50 \times 50$ cm), water types 5–6, 77–81°F (25–27°C).

Care: Keep one male with several females in tanks with sandy areas and a few rock structures to swim through. Eats all standard foods.

Habits: Eats other fish. Found in the transition zone between rocks and sand in Lake Malawi. Not pair-forming; maternal mouthbrooder.

Compatibility: Keep with other Lake Malawi cichlids that do not inhabit rocky areas, such as *Copadichromis* or *Aulonocara*.

100 gal

Electric Blue Johanni *Melanochromis johannii*

Also: Bluegray Mbuna, johanni cichlid

Family: Cichlids, Cichlidae (see page 10).

Characteristics: 5 in (12 cm), male has blue-black stripes.

Tank/Water: $40 \times 20 \times 20$ in ($100 \times 50 \times 50$ cm), water types 5–6, 77–81°F (25–27°C).

Care: Rock structures piled so as to allow the fish to swim through. Plant-based flaked food and frozen food containing crustaceans. Keep one or many males with several females.

Habits: Rock-dwelling Lake Malawi cichlid (Mbuna); distribution restricted to a small area of the lake. Eats algae, small animals, also plankton. Maternal mouthbrooder; does not form pairs.

Compatibility: With other Lake Malawi rock cichlids.

62.5 gal

Elongated Lemon Cichlid *Neolamprologus longior*
Also: Tanganyikan lemon cichlid, *Neolamprologus leleupi*
Family: Cichlids, Cichlidae (see page 10).
Characteristics: 4 in (10 cm), females stay somewhat smaller, males develop a small forehead bump in old age.
Tank/Water: $40 \times 16 \times 16$ in ($100 \times 40 \times 40$ cm), water types 5–6, 77–81°F (25–27°C).

37.5 gal

Care: Keep in pairs in tanks with stone structures that offer crevices and caves as hiding places. Feed crustacean-based food, such as shrimp mixes; *Artemia* will keep the beautiful yellow color bright.
Habits: Lives hidden in caves of the rock zone in Lake Tanganyika. Pair-forming cavity brooder.
Compatibility: With other cichlids from Lake Tanganyika.

Ember Tetra *Hyphessobrycon amandae*
Family: Tetras, Characidae (see page 16).
Characteristics: 1 in (3 cm) male slimmer and smaller.
Tank/Water: $24 \times 12 \times 12$ in ($60 \times 30 \times 30$ cm), water types 1–3, 76–83°F (24–28°C).
Care: Keep this schooling fish (10–30 specimens) in tanks with

12.5 gal

a dark substrate and dense vegetation. Feed all small foods (such as *Cyclops*, *Artemia* nauplii, dry foods). The intense red color appears only in soft, acid water with peat filtration. In hard, alkaline water the life span is short.
Habits: Known to be native only to a blackwater stream in the Mato Grosso region of Brazil.
Compatibility: Only with other dwarf species.

Emerald Catfish *Brochis splendens*
Family: Callichthyid armored catfish, Callichthyidae (see page 9).
Characteristics: 3 in (8 cm), male slimmer.
Tank/Water: $40 \times 20 \times 20$ in ($100 \times 50 \times 50$ cm), water types 2–5, 74–81°F (23–27°C).
Care: As a group in tanks with a large surface area and some large-leaved plants and roots as shelters. Sand substrate in

62.5 gal

parts. Feed food tablets and frozen small crustaceans.
Habits: Group fish found in slow-flowing, shallow, often muddy waters in the Amazon area, South America.
Compatibility: Peaceful companion for all South American fish of the same tank region, such as discus, angelfish, characins, and "root-dwelling" suckermouth armored catfish (*Ancistrus* species).

Emperor Tetra *Nematobrycon palmeri*

Family: Tetras, Characidae (see page 16).
Characteristics: 2.4 in (6 cm), male more colorful, female plumper.
Tank/Water: 32 × 14 × 16 in (80 × 35 × 40 cm), water types 2–5, 74–79°F (23–26°C).

25 gal

Care: Group fish for loosely planted, dark aquariums. Always keep several males, as some may become aggressive toward other aquarium tenants. All smaller foods, plant foods.
Habits: Native to Colombian streams and rivers. The males occasionally become rough, because they defend spawning territories against other males.
Compatibility: Best with lively, but nonterritorial fish (other characins, armored catfish).

Enantiopus melanogenys

Family: Cichlids, Cichlidae (see page 10).
Characteristics: 6 in (15 cm), male more colorful in spawning period.
Tank/Water: 48 × 24 × 20 in (120 × 60 × 50 cm), water types 5–6, 77–81°F (25–27°C).

87.5 gal

Care: Spacious tanks with sand substrate and no other furnishings. Varied diet of different fine frozen and dry foods. Keep a group of seven specimens, including two or three males.
Habits: Found in schools above pure sandy bottoms in Lake Tanganyika. At spawning time the males change color and dig spawning pits in the sand. Maternal mouthbrooder; not pair-forming.
Compatibility: Cichlids (*Cyprichromis*).

Endler's Guppy *Poecilia sp. "Endler's"*

Family: Live-bearing toothcarp, Poeciliidae (see page 20).
Characteristics: 2 in (5 cm), male has copulatory organ.
Tank/Water: 24 × 12 × 12 in (60 × 30 × 30 cm), water types 4–6, 79–83°F (26–28°C).

12.5 gal

Care: Keep at least three pairs in a well-planted, brightly lit, sufficiently warm aquarium, with a cover of floating plants in parts. Feed dry food, frozen or live *Artemia* nauplii.
Habits: Thus far known to be indigenous only to a single freshwater lagoon in northeastern Venezuela that was clouded with green floating algae. Maximum life span of two years. The species may have become extinct in the wild.
Compatibility: With bottom-oriented small fish that tolerate hard water, such as *Corydoras hastatus*.

Eye-Spot Rasbora *Rasbora dorsiocellata*

Family: Carp and minnows, Cyprinidae (see page 16).
Characteristics: 2.4 in (6 cm), female plumper.
Tank/Water: 24 × 12 × 12 in (60 × 30 × 30 cm), water types 2–5, 74–83°F (23–28°C).

12.5 gal

Care: Ideal schooling fish for tanks that are densely planted in parts. Feed all smaller foods, such as insect larvae and dry foods.
Habits: Native to Southeast Asia (Malaysia and Indonesia).
Compatibility: With smaller fish also from still waters in Asia, such as dwarf or honey gouramis, fiveband barbs, and small *Botia* species.
Similar species: *Rasbora macrophthalma* looks almost identical, but stays much smaller: 1.4 in (3.5 cm).

Fairy Cichlid *Aulonocara jacobfreibergi*

Family: Cichlids, Cichlidae (see page 10).
Characteristics: 5.5 in (14 cm), female colorless and smaller.
Tank/Water: 48 × 20 × 20 in (120 × 50 × 50 cm), water types 5–6, 79–81°F (25–27°C).

75 gal

Care: Peaceful species. Keep one male and several females in dark tanks with sand substrate and roomy caves. Feed all foods, especially shrimp-rich foods.
Habits: Large caves at the interface between rock and sand in Lake Malawi. Maternal mouthbrooder; not pair-forming.
Compatibility: Best with sand or freshwater Lake Malawi cichlids, but not with the highly competitive rock-dwelling species such as *Melanochromis*.

Featherfin Catfish *Synodontis cf. eupterus*

Family: Naked catfish, Mochokidae (see page 9).
Characteristics: 8.6 in (22 cm), hard to sex.
Tank/Water: 80 × 24 × 24 in (200 × 60 × 60 cm), water types 2–5, 79–85°F (26–29°C).

175 gal

Care: Large tanks with roots as hiding places and sandy bottom in parts. Feed all standard foods, also dry foods containing plant matter. Keep single specimen or larger group. Powerful filter.
Habits: Peaceful species mostly found in cloudy waters of West Africa. Species hard to classify.
Compatibility: With other West African species, such as African red-eyed characins, Peter's elephant noses, or tilapias (*Tilapia joka*).

Featherfin Cichlid *Cyathopharynx furcifer*

Family: Cichlids, Cichlidae (see page 10).

Characteristics: 8.25 in (21 cm), female smaller and colorless.

Tank/Water: 80 × 24 × 24 in (200 × 60 × 60 cm), water types 5–6, 77–81°F (25–27°C).

175 gal

Care: Keep one male with several females in tanks with few rocks, plenty of swimming space, and a sandy substrate. Takes all standard foods, also *Artemia*.

Habits: Intermediate zone between sand and rocks in Lake Tanganyika, where it eats small food particles in open water or from the rock surface. Maternal mouthbrooder; does not form pairs.

Compatibility: In large tanks with *Paracyprichromis* and *Cyphotilapia frontosa*.

Figure Eight Puffer *Tetraodon biocellatus*

Family: Puffers, Tetraodontidae (see page 20).

Characteristics: 2.4 in (6 cm), hard to sex. This small species, unlike the other, much larger, green-spotted puffers *T. fluviatilis* and *T. nigroventris*, has two black eye-shaped spots at the base of the dorsal fin.

Tank/Water: 24 × 12 × 12 in (60 × 30 × 30 cm), water types 4–6, 76–83°F (24–28°C).

12.5 gal

Care: Singly in small tanks furnished with lots of structures. Eats only live foods (also snails).

Habits: Pure freshwater species native to Southeast Asia.

Compatibility: Best in a species tank, possibly with fast-swimming species such as robust barbs, which are not bothered by the puffers.

Fire Spiny Eel *Mastacembelus favus*

Family: Spiny eels, Mastacembelidae (see page 21).

Characteristics: 28 in (70 cm), female plumper.

Tank/Water: 80 × 24 × 20 in (200 × 60 × 50 cm), water types 2–5, 77–85°F (25–29°C).

150 gal

Care: Keep singly or as a group in tanks with water movement and fine gravelly substrate, into which they can burrow. Caves as hiding places. Accepts high-nutrient live and frozen foods.

Habits: Nocturnal predator of insects and crustaceans in sometimes fast-flowing lowland rivers in Southeast Asia. After a while, these intelligent creatures will give up their habit of hiding and become trusting.

Compatibility: Because of their predatory ways, only with larger high-backed species, such as large barbs.

Fire Stingray *Potamotrygon henlei*
Family: Freshwater stingrays, Potamotrygonidae (see page 6).
Characteristics: Disc diameter at least 24 in (60 cm). Poison spine at end of whiptail—danger of injury. Males and females have different anal fins.
Tank/Water: 160 × 60 × 24 in (400 × 150 × 60 cm), water types 2–5, 81–85°F (27–29°C).
Care: Keep in pairs in tanks with at least a 2.5-in (6-cm) layer of sand and strong filtration. No sharp-edged rocks or rod-type heaters in the tank—the rays might hurt themselves. Feed large quantities of clams, mussels, and frozen shrimp.
Habits: Sandy banks of the Rio Xingu in Brazil.
Compatibility: With other large South American fish such as oscars, green arowanas, silver dollars.

875 gal

Firemouth Cichlid *Thorichthys meeki*
Also: *Cichlasoma meeki*
Family: Cichlids, Cichlidae (see page 10).
Characteristics: 6 in (15 cm), male larger, has longer fins.
Tank/Water: 48 × 24 × 24 in (120 × 60 × 60 cm), water types 3–6, 76–81°F (24–27°C).
Care: Keep a group of six specimens; pairs will form intermittently. Furnish tank correspondingly, with roots and large plants to create territorial boundaries. Feed small crustaceans and high-fiber dry foods. No red mosquito larvae!
Habits: Shallow areas with rocks or embedded wood near banks of various rivers in Mexico and Guatemala. Pair-forming open spawner.
Compatibility: Good with large swordtails.

100 gal

Firemouth Killifish *Epiplatys dageti*
Family: Killifish, Aplocheilidae (see page 19).
Characteristics: 2.4 in (6 cm), male larger and more colorful.
Tank/Water: 24 × 12 × 12 in (60 × 30 × 30 cm), water types 2–5, 74–79°F (23–26°C).
Care: Planted aquariums with cover of floating plants in parts. Feed insect foods, other small live foods, and dry foods as well. Keep several males with many females.
Habits: Insect-eating surface fish native to waters that are plant-rich in parts, in the swampy coastal lowlands of Liberia and Ivory Coast.
Compatibility: Ideal companion fish for West African dwarf cichlids (such as *Pelvicachromis*), smaller characins (such as *Neolebias*), and barbs.

12.5 gal

Fiveband Barb *Puntius pentazona*

Also: Six-banded tiger barb
Family: Carp and minnows, Cyprinidae (see page 16).
Characteristics: About 2 in (5 cm), female plumper.
Tank/Water: 24 × 12 × 12 in (60 × 30 × 30 cm), water types 1–3, 79–85°F (26–29°C).
Care: Keep as a group (of at least six specimens) in dark tanks with peat filtration, soft, not sharp-edged substrate, and loose plantings of *Cryptocoryne*. Root shelters. All foods.
Habits: Group fish that lives near the bottom of blackwater areas in Southeast Asia; "grazes" on soft bottom, seeking food.
Compatibility: Good companion for moderately lively fish with identical water requirements, such as *Rasbora* species, gouramis, and loaches (such as *Pangio*).

12.5 gal

Five-banded Killifish *Aphyosemion striatum*

Family: Killifish, family Aplocheilidae (see page 19).
Characteristics: 2 in (5 cm), male bigger and more colorful.
Tank/Water: 24 × 12 × 12 in (60 × 30 × 30 cm), water types 2–5, 70–74°F (21–23°C).
Care: Keep several males with many females in small, dark tanks. Small roots and plant groups provide territorial boundaries and retreats for defeated males or females too hotly pursued by males. Live and dry foods.
Habits: Insect eater found in extremely shallow areas near banks of tiny rain forest streams in northern Gabon.
Compatibility: Some killifish (such as *Epiplatys sexfasciatus*), African barbs (such as *Barbus barilioides*), or lampeyes (such as *Procatopus*).

12.5 gal

Flag Cichlid *Mesonauta insignis*

Family: Cichlids, Cichlidae (see page 10).
Characteristics: 8 in (20 cm), females stay smaller.
Tank/Water: 48 × 20 × 20 in (120 × 50 × 50 cm), water types 2–5, 76–86°F (24–30°C).
Care: Keep in pairs in tanks with large-leaved plants and roots that reach all the way to the water surface. Feed all standard foods.
Habits: Lives near surface in waters of northern Amazon region, found in places in black water characterized by dead wood or plant growth. Pair-forming open spawner.
Compatibility: With other peaceful South American cichlids, such as Uaru cichlids, discus, angelfish.
Similar species: *Mesonauta festivus,* 8 in (20 cm).

75 gal

Flagtail Cory *Corydoras robineae*

Family: Callichthyid armored catfish, Callichthyidae (see page 9).
Characteristics: 2.75 in (7 cm), female plumper.
Tank/Water: 32 × 14 × 16 in (80 × 35 × 40 cm), water types 2–4, 76–83°F (24–28°C).

25 gal

Care: Keep as a group in tanks with sandy substrate in parts, loose plantings, and structures where they can go to rest. Feed fine live, frozen, and dry foods. Use specifically labeled foods for *Corydoras*!
Habits: Gregarious fish found in sandy waters of a tributary of the Rio Negro in Brazil.
Compatibility: Ideal companion for South American fish of the middle and upper tank regions. In small tanks, not suitable with cichlids; in larger tanks, also with discus and angelfish.

Flag-tailed Porthole Catfish *Dianema urostriatum*

Also: *Dianema urostriata*

Family: Callyichthyid armored catfish, Callichthyidae (see page 9).
Characteristics: 4 in (10 cm), female plumper and larger.
Tank/Water: 40 × 20 × 20 in (100 × 50 × 50 cm), water types 2–5, 77–83°F (25–28°C).

62.5 gal

Care: Keep a group of about six specimens in dark tanks with floating plants and plenty of hiding places. Feed live, frozen, and dry foods.
Habits: Gregarious species, able, like all other callyichthids, to breathe atmospheric oxygen through its intestines. Often found in pools of residual water from the Rio Negro near Manaus (Brazil).
Compatibility: With peaceful fish of the same tank region.

Flame Tetra *Hyphessobrycon flammeus*

Family: Tetras, Characidae (see page 16).
Characteristics: 1.5 in (4 cm), female paler and plumper.
Tank/Water: 24 × 12 × 12 in (60 × 30 × 30 cm), water types 3–6, 72–81°F (22–27°C).

12.5 gal

Care: Group fish (at least six to eight specimens) for dark, loosely to densely planted aquariums. Takes all smaller foods. Should be kept warmer than 76–77°F (24–25°C) only temporarily.
Habits: Found in streams near Rio de Janeiro.
Compatibility: With smaller bottom and surface fish that tolerate somewhat cooler water, such as peppered catfish (*Corydoras paleatus*), Borelli's dwarf cichlid (*Apistogramma borellii*).
Similar species: Yellow tetra, *H. bifasciatus,* 2 in (5 cm).

Forktail Blue-Eye *Pseudomugil furcatus*
Also: *Popondetta furcata, Popondichthys furcatus*
Family: Blue-eyes, Pseudomugilidae (see page 18).
Characteristics: 2.5 in (6 cm), male more colorful, has larger fins.
Tank/Water: 24 × 12 × 12 in (60 × 30 × 30 cm), water types 3–5, 76–81°F (24–27°C).

12.5 gal

Care: Tanks with plenty of water movement, plantings along sides, and rocky bottom. Individual bunches of Java moss. Keep a few males with several females. Small live, frozen, and dry foods.
Habits: Lively group fish found in fast-flowing streams with rocky bottoms in northern New Guinea.
Compatibility: With small fish from stream bottoms.

Frog-mouthed Catfish *Chaca bankanensis*
Family: Frog-mouthed catfish, Chacidae (see page 9).
Characteristics: 8 in (20 cm), hard to sex.
Tank/Water: 32 × 14 × 16 in (80 × 35 × 40 cm), water types 2–5, 74–79°F (23–26°C).

25 gal

Care: Keep singly in shallow tanks with some structures, such as a bog-pine root and individual plants. Feed highly nutritious diet of live food fish, such as golden orf or small goldfish.
Habits: Well-camouflaged lurking predator found in virgin-forest waters in Southeast Asia. Eats quite large fish more than half its own length, and shrimp.
Compatibility: The species should not be kept in a community tank because smaller fish up to about 6 in (15 cm) will be eaten, and larger fish will eat all their food.

Frontosa Cichlid *Cyphotilapia frontosa*
Family: Cichlids, Cichlidae (see page 10).
Characteristics: 10 in (33 cm), male has longer fins.
Tank/Water: 80 × 24 × 24 in (200 × 60 × 60 cm), water types 5–6, 77–81°F (25–27°C).

175 gal

Care: Peaceful species; keep two males with several females in tanks with a few roomy caves. Feed shrimp and frozen fish.
Habits: Fish eater found in Lake Tanganyika, eats mainly small cichlids that sleep at night (such as *Cyprichromis*). Sometimes forms groups. Maternal mouthbrooder; does not form pairs.
Compatibility: With larger Lake Tanganyikan cichlids (such as *Cyathopharynx*) and *Synodontis multipunctatus*.

Garnet Tetra *Hemigrammus pulcher*

Family: Tetras, Characidae (see page 16).
Characteristics: 1.78 in (4.5 cm), male less plump.
Tank/Water: 24 × 12 × 12 in (60 × 30 × 30 cm), water types 1–2, 74–83°F (23–28°C).

12.5 gal

Care: Demanding tetra where water values are concerned (peat filtration is best); its delicate, iridescent pastel colors are effective only in dark tanks with dense plantings in parts. Feed fine live food (such as black mosquito larvae), but also frozen and dry foods. Keep at least six specimens.
Habits: Probably native to blackwater streams and flooded forests of the Peruvian Amazon.
Compatibility: Good companion for demanding softwater fish, such as *Dicrossus filamentosus*.

Geophagus cf. *altifrons*

Also: *Geophagus surinamensis*
Family: Cichlids, Cichlidae (see page 10).
Characteristics: 10 in (25 cm), male has longer fins.
Tank/Water: 60 × 24 × 24 in (150 × 60 × 60 cm), water types 2–5, 81–86°F (27–30°C).

125 gal

Care: Keep six to eight specimens in tanks with sand substrate and only a few structures in the tank background. Only robust plants. Accepts all standard foods.
Habits: Sandy, muddy, gravelly, or rocky areas of large rivers in Amazonia (often near wood deposits). Usually pair-forming mouthbrooder.
Compatibility: Good with silver dollars, suckermouth armored catfish, and peaceful large cichlids such as *Heros*.

Giant Danio *Devario aequipinnatus*

Also: *Danio aequipinnatus*
Family: Carp and minnows, Cyprinidae (see page 16).
Characteristics: 4 in (10 cm), female plumper.
Tank/Water: 48 × 16 × 20 in (120 × 40 × 50 cm), water types 2–6, 76–81°F (24–27°C).

62.5 gal

Care: Species for the area near the surface of bright, large tanks with plenty of swimming space. Feed all standard foods, especially small flying insects. Keep at least six to eight specimens.
Habits: Gregarious, current-loving stream and river fish found in Peninsular India and Sri Lanka. Eats insects.
Compatibility: Ideal with bottom-dwelling stream fish from Asia, such as stream loaches (*Schistura*, *Nemacheilus*) or hill-stream loaches (*Gastromyzon*).

Giant Whiptail Catfish *Pseudohemiodon laticeps*
Family: Suckermouth armored catfish, Loricariidae (see page 9).
Characteristics: 12 in (30 cm), male has "whiskerlike" barbels.
Tank/Water: $60 \times 24 \times 12$ in ($150 \times 60 \times 30$ cm), water types 3–5, 77–83°F (25–28°C).

62.5 gal

Care: Keep a pair or one male with several females in spacious tanks with pure sand substrate. Only a few structures should break up the sandy bottom zone. Varied diet of tablets, red mosquito larvae, frozen *Cyclops*, or water fleas.
Habits: Small-animal eater found in sandy areas of the Paraná River in southern South America. Often burrows into the sand.
Compatibility: Only with fish of the upper tank regions. Bottom dwellers (callichthyid armored catfish) not suitable.
Similar species: *Pseudohemiodon lamina*, 8 in (20 cm).

Glass Bloodfin *Prionobrama filigera*
Family: Tetras, Characidae (see page 16).
Characteristics: 2 in (5 cm), female plumper and less colorful.
Tank/Water: $32 \times 14 \times 16$ in ($80 \times 35 \times 40$ cm), water types 3–6, 74–81°F (23–27°C).

25 gal

Care: In brightly lit aquariums with loose plantings along the sides and low water movement. Feed all standard foods. Buy at least eight specimens.
Habits: Lively schooling fish, which is caught, for example, along the sandy banks of largish rivers in South America. Probably eats insects found on the water surface.
Compatibility: Unproblematic with smaller South American fish that are not dependent on extremely soft water (water type 1), such as callichthyid armored catfish, and whiptail loricaria.

Glass Catfish *Kryptopterus minor*
Also: Ghost catfish, *Kryptopterus bicirrhis*
Family: True catfish, Siluridae (see page 9).
Characteristics: 3 in (8 cm), female plumper.
Tank/Water: $40 \times 16 \times 16$ in ($100 \times 40 \times 40$ cm), water types 2–5, 76–83°F (24–28°C).

37.5 gal

Care: Gregarious species that loves to swim: Keep at least 6-10 specimens in tanks with plenty of structures, loose plantings, floating plants, and gentle water movement. Feed fine and medium-sized live food; reluctant to eat frozen or dry foods.
Habits: Schooling fish native to weed-filled, slow-moving flowing waters of Southeast Asia. Diet unknown.
Compatibility: Cypriniforms of the genus *Rasbora*, such as *Rasbora dorsiocellata*, and loaches, such as *Botia striata*.

Glowlight Rasbora *Trigonostigma hengeli*
Also: *Rasbora hengeli*
Family: Carp and minnows, Cyprinidae (see page 16).
Characteristics: 1.4 in (3.5 cm), male has larger wedge-shaped spot.
Tank/Water: 24 × 12 × 12 in (60 × 30 × 30 cm), water types 1–3, 77–83°F (25–28°C).

12.5 gal

Care: Blackwater tanks with dark substrate, loosely planted with *Cryptocoryne* (peat filtration or peat extract as additive). Takes all smaller foods, loves black mosquito larvae. Keep only in a school of at least 8-10 specimens.
Habits: Schooling fish found in the blackwater swamps of Indonesia, where they probably eat insects.
Compatibility: Labyrinthfish, loaches, and slimmer rasboras.

Glowlight Tetra *Hemigrammus erythrozonus*
Family: Tetras, Characidae (see page 16).
Characteristics: Up to about 1.5 in (4 cm), female plumper.
Tank/Water: 24 × 12 × 12 in (60 × 30 × 30 cm), water types 1–5, 74–79°F (23–26°C).

12.5 gal

Care: Peaceful schooling fish (at least 8–10 specimens) for dark tanks with loose plantings and floating plants. The subdued colors are most effective in peat-filtered water with a dark substrate. Feed smaller foods.
Habits: Lives in loose groups in virgin-forest streams of the Essequibo River system in Guyana, South America.
Compatibility: With small, peaceful fish that also prefer dark tanks, such as other tetras (such as *Nannostomus* pencilfish) and small catfish (*Corydoras*).

Gold Nugget Pleco *Baryancistrus sp.*
Also: L18, big white-spot pleco
Family: Suckermouth armored catfish, Loricariidae (see page 9).
Characteristics: At least 14 in (35 cm), male has flatter, wider head, while female's head is rounder. The pretty coloration of the juveniles disappears in adulthood.
Tank/Water: 128 × 24 × 24 in (320 × 60 × 60 cm), water types 3–5, 79–85°F (26–29°C).

300 gal

Care: Keep one or several in large aquariums with roots and large stones. Feed plant foods and plant-based dry food pellets.
Habits: They graze on the algae and microorganisms found on stones and roots in the Rio Xingu, Brazil.
Compatibility: Peaceful large cichlids.
Similar species: L47 *Baryancistrus sp.* "Magnum," 12 in (30 cm).

Gold Tetra *Hemigrammus rodwayi*
Also: *Hemigrammus armstrongi*
Family: Tetras, Characidae (see page 16).
Characteristics: 1.5 in (4 cm), female plumper in the abdominal region. The gold coloration is caused by harmless skin parasites that produce a characteristic skin reaction in characins. Thus parasite-free progeny often are colorless.

12.5 gal

Tank/Water: 24 × 12 × 12 in (60 × 30 × 30 cm), water types 2–5, 76–81°F (24–27°C).
Care: Schooling fish for aquariums that are densely planted in parts. Feed frozen or live small crustaceans, black mosquito larvae, also dry foods.
Habits: Common in small streams of the Amazon basin.
Compatibility: Small bottom fish and characins.

Golden Barb *Puntius semifasciolatus "schuberti"*
Family: Carp and minnows, Cyprinidae (see page 16).
Characteristics: 2.75 in (7 cm), female plumper. Cultivated form.
Tank/Water: 32 × 14 × 16 in (80 × 35 × 40 cm), water types 2–6, 68–76°F (20–24°C).

25 gal

Care: Loosely planted, well-lit tank with sufficient space to swim. At least in parts, soft substrate for burrowing. Undemanding where food is concerned.
Habits: Lively group fish (keep at least six specimens) of the bottom region; has no natural habitat since it is a cultivated form.
Compatibility: Good to put with other lively fish that prefer cooler temperatures, such as rosy barbs or *Xenoteca eiseni*.

Golden-eyed Dwarf Cichlid *Nannacara anomala*
Family: Cichlids, Cichlidae (see page 10).
Characteristics: 3 in (8 cm), male bigger and more colorful.
Tank/Water: 32 × 14 × 16 in (80 × 35 × 40 cm), water types 1–4, 77–83°F (25–28°C).
Care: Keep in pairs in densely planted tanks with lots of structures, including some caves to hide in. Feed all standard foods.

25 gal

Habits: Slow-flowing or standing, vegetation-rich water bodies in northeastern South America. Pair-forming open spawner or cavity brooder.
Compatibility: Characins, such as rosy tetras or hatchetfish. Also suckermouth armored catfish, such as *Ancistrus*, that are too big to enter the caves.
Similar species: *Nannacara aureocephalus*, 3.5 in (9 cm).

119

Gray Bichir *Polypterus senegalus*
Also: Senegal bichir
Family: Bichirs, Polypteridae (see page 6).
Characteristics: 12 in (30 cm), male has larger anal fin.
Tank/Water: 48 × 20 × 20 in (120 × 50 × 50 cm), water types 2–6, 77–85°F (25–29°C).

75 gal

Care: Keep in pairs or in groups in large tanks with hiding places (such as roots). Takes all highly nutritious live and frozen foods.
Habits: Nocturnal predator of shrimp and small fish in the swamps, rivers, and lakes of West Africa. Juveniles up to 4 in (10 cm), like all other bichirs, have feathery external gills and resemble salamander larvae.
Compatibility: Only with larger fish, such as *Synodontis*.

Green Knifefish *Eigenmannia sp.*
Also: Glass knifefish, *Eigenmannia lineata*
Family: Knifefish, Sternopygidae (see page 8).
Characteristics: 14.5–18 in (35–45 cm), depending on species, male much larger, female has plumper belly.
Tank/Water: 100 × 24 × 24 in (250 × 60 × 60 cm), water types 2–5, 77–85°F (25–29°C).

225 gal

Care: Group fish: one male with four or five females in roomy tanks with cover of floating plants (such as water lettuce in strongly lit tanks). Feed live and frozen mosquito larvae.
Habits: These gregarious species live beneath "floating meadows," that is, under patches of floating plants, in South America. They use electric signals for orientation and communication.
Compatibility: Peaceful bottom fish native to South America.

Green Neon Tetra *Paracheirodon simulans*
Family: Tetras, Characidae (see page 16).
Characteristics: 1.4 in (3.5 cm), female plumper. Distinguished from the cardinal tetra by the less clearly defined red and white areas on its abdomen.
Tank/Water: 24 × 12 × 12 in (60 × 30 × 30 cm), water types 1–3, 77–83°F (25–28°C).

12.5 gal

Care: In dark tanks with abundant plant growth. Feed fine live, frozen, and dry foods. Keep at least 15–20 specimens together.
Habits: Thus far identified only in relatively warm, clear stream sections that widened into pondlike areas in the upper Rio Negro in Brazil.
Compatibility: Ideally only with dainty fish such as dwarf pencilfish and small *Corydoras* species.

Guppy *Poecilia reticulata*
Also: Millions fish, *Lebistes reticulates*
Family: Live-bearing toothcarp of the family Poeciliidae (see page 20).
Characteristics: About 2.4 in (6 cm), male has copulatory organ.
Tank/Water: 24 × 12 × 12 in (60 × 30 × 30 cm), water types 2–5, 76–86°F (24–30°C).
Care: As a group in tanks that are densely planted in parts. Varied diet including all smaller foods, also plant matter.
Habits: Standing and gently flowing waters of northern South America. Released into the wild worldwide.
Compatibility: With small catfish, characins, and dwarf cichlids. Best kept as single species or only with bottom fish.

12.5 gal

Guyana Eye-Spot Cichlid *Heros notatus "Guyana"*
Family: Cichlids, Cichlidae (see page 10).
Characteristics: 10 in (25 cm), male larger and somewhat more colorful.
Tank/Water: 60 × 24 × 24 in (150 × 60 × 60 cm), water types 2–5, 77–85°F (25–29°C).
Care: Keep this species in pairs, which will be at home in dark tanks with many roots as shelters. Feed standard foods; green foods are important.
Habits: Primarily herbivorous cichlids native to the waters of Guyana's Rupununi wet savannah. Usually pair-forming open spawner.
Compatibility: With other peaceful large cichlids, such as *Geophagus* species, but with silver dollars as well.

137.5 gal

Harlequin Rasbora *Trigonostigma heteromorpha*
Also: *Rasbora heteromorpha*
Family: Carp and minnows, Cyprinidae (see page 16).
Characteristics: About 1.75 in (4.5 cm), female plumper.
Tank/Water: 24 × 12 × 12 in (60 × 30 × 30 cm), water types 2–5, 74–83°F (23–28°C).
Care: Dark, blackwater tank (peat filtration or peat extract as additive), loosely planted with *Cryptocoryne*. Takes all smaller foods, likes black mosquito larvae. Keep only in a school of 8–10 specimens.
Habits: Schooling fish found in the blackwater swamps and streams of Malaysia, where it probably eats insects.
Compatibility: With labyrinthfish, loaches, and slimmer rasboras, such as red-striped rasboras.

12.5 gal

High-backed Headstander *Abramites hypselonotus*
Family: Headstanders, Anostomidae (see page 16).
Characteristics: 5.5 in (14 cm), no known sex differences.
Tank/Water: $64 \times 24 \times 24$ in ($160 \times 60 \times 60$ cm), water types 2–5, 77–83°F (25–28°C).
Care: If singly kept, may bully other fish, so keep at least five specimens in a dark aquarium furnished with plenty of roots. Needs green foods, also plant-based dry foods.
Habits: Herbivorous and sometimes territorial characin widely found in the Amazon River basin in South America. Likes to hide among pieces of dead wood.
Compatibility: Good companion fish for South American giant cichlids and suckermouth armored catfish.
Similar species: *Abramites solarii*, 5 in (12 cm).

125 gal

Hogchoker *Trinectes maculates*
Also: *Achirus fasciatus*
Family: American soles, Achiridae (see page 20).
Characteristics: 8 in (20 cm), no sexual differences known.
Tank/Water: $48 \times 24 \times 20$ in ($120 \times 60 \times 50$ cm), water types 6–7, 65–76°F (18–24°C).
Care: Spacious tanks with sand substrate for burrowing. Feed tubifex, mosquito larvae, food tablets.
Habits: Marine species whose range also extends far into fresh water; most imports come from Florida.
Compatibility: With peaceful, not overly small fish of the middle and upper tank regions.
Remarks: Other freshwater soles are imported from Asia and South America. Some are true freshwater fish and stay smaller.

87.5 gal

Honey Gourami *Colisa chuna*
Also: *Colisa sota*
Family: Gouramis, Osphronemidae (see page 16).
Characteristics: 2 in (5 cm), males ready to mate display full color. Otherwise hard to sex.
Tank/Water: $24 \times 12 \times 12$ in ($60 \times 30 \times 30$ cm), water types 2–6, 72–83°F (22–28°C).
Care: Keep in pairs in densely planted tanks with cover of floating plants. Feed all standard small foods. Usually colorless in dealer's tank.
Habits: Peaceful fish that displays its full splendor only when in a mating mood. Native to areas near banks and flood areas of slow-flowing or standing waters in northeastern India.
Compatibility: Only with delicate fish such as *Badis*.

12.5 gal

Jumbo Coolie *Pangio myersi*

Family: Loaches, Cobitidae (see page 17).

Characteristics: About 4 in (10 cm), hard to sex. Be careful—there are spines beneath its eyes!

Tank/Water: 24 × 12 × 12 in (60 × 30 × 30 cm), water types 2–5, 76–86°F (24–30°C).

12.5 gal

Care: Keep several specimens in densely planted (Java moss cushions), dark (cover of floating plants) tanks. Soft substrate. Feed small live, frozen, and dry foods.

Habits: In vegetation-rich streams and standing waters in Thailand. Nocturnal fish that hide in the daytime. In an aquarium they show themselves during the day as well.

Compatibility: Barbs and labyrinthfish native to Asia.

"Kadango Red" *Copadichromis borleyi "Kadango red"*

Family: Cichlids, Cichlidae (see page 10).

Characteristics: 5.5 in (14 cm), female smaller and colorless.

Tank/Water: 64 × 24 × 24 in (160 × 60 × 60 cm), water types 5–6, 77–81°F (25–27°C).

150 gal

Care: One male with several females, with lots of open swimming space and some rocks. Feed all foods; food containing crustaceans (*Cyclops*, *Artemia*, shrimp mixes) is important in order to maintain coloring.

Habits: One of Lake Malawi's few plankton eaters; prefers to live near rock habitats. Maternal mouthbrooder; does not form pairs.

Compatibility: With Lake Malawi cichlids from open water, sand, or cave biotopes. Not good with rock-dwelling species.

Kenyi Cichlid *Metriaclima lombardoi*

Also: *Pseudotropheus lombardoi, Maylandia kombardoi*

Family: Cichlids, Cichlidae (see page 10).

Characteristics: 6 in (15 cm), adult males are yellow, while females have blue body color.

Tank/Water: 64 × 24 × 24 in (160 × 60 × 60 cm), water types 5–6, 77–81°F (25–27°C).

150 gal

Care: Keep one or many males with several females. Pile up rocks so that the fish can swim through them. Feed plant-based dry foods and small crustaceans (live or frozen).

Habits: Algae and plankton eater found in the rock zone of Lake Malawi. Maternal mouthbrooder.

Compatibility: With other Lake Malawi cichlids, such as *Pseudotropheus* or *Metriaclima* species.

Lamp-eyed Panchax *Aplocheilichthys macrophthalmus*

Also: *A. luxophthalmus, Poropanchax macrophthalmus*
Family: Lampeyes, family Poeciliidae (see page 20).
Characteristics: 1.4 in (3.5 cm), male has more colorful fins.
Tank/Water: 24 × 12 × 12 in (60 × 30 × 30 cm), water types 2–5, 77–83°F (25–28°C).
Care: Keep at least 10 specimens in dark tanks that are densely planted in parts and have slight water movement. Fine live or dry foods.
Habits: Schooling fish found in quiet areas of medium-sized and large flowing waters in the rain forests of Cameroon and Nigeria.
Compatibility: With small West African dwarf cichlids (such as *Pelvicachromis*) or *Aphyosemion*.

12.5 gal

Least Rasbora *Boraras urophthalmoides*

Also: Exclamation-point rasbora, *Rasbora urophthalma*
Family: Carp and minnows, Cyprinidae (see page 16).
Characteristics: .75 in (2 cm), female plumper.
Tank/Water: 24 × 12 × 12 in (60 × 30 × 30 cm), water types 2–5, 76–79°F (24–26°C).
Care: This robust *Boraras* species can easily be kept in densely planted aquariums in a largish school (20–30 specimens). Feed finest live foods, such as *Artemia,* but fine dry foods are also good.
Habits: Indigenous primarily to swamps and ponds in Southeast Asia with fine-leaved aquatic plants.
Compatibility: With all dwarf fish of the lower tank strata that prefer similar water values, such as *Pangio kuhlii*.

12.5 gal

Lemon Tetra *Hyphessobrycon pulchripinnis*

Family: Tetras, Characidae (see page 16).
Characteristics: 1.75 in (4.5 cm), female plumper.
Tank/Water: 24 × 12 × 12 in (60 × 30 × 30 cm), water types 2–4, 76–81°F (24–27°C).
Care: Schooling fish (keep at least six specimens) for aquariums that are densely planted in parts. The intense yellow coloring, from which this fish gets its name, is promoted by a diet of small crustaceans (*Cyclops, Artemia* nauplii) and can be maintained only in soft, slightly acid water.
Habits: Plant-rich clearwater streams.
Compatibility: In larger tanks, also with dwarf cichlids and angelfish; in small ones, only with other characins and suckermouth and callyichthid armored catfish.

12.5 gal

Lima Shovelnose Catfish *Sorubim lima*
Family: Long-whiskered catfish, Pimelodidae (see page 9).
Characteristics: 21 in (53 cm), hard to sex.
Tank/Water: 128 × 24 × 24 in (320 × 60 × 60 cm), water types 2–5, 76–85°F (24–29°C).
Care: As a group in large tanks with roots and large-leaved plants as shelters. Feed nutritious diet of live or dead fish.
Habits: This nocturnal species from the large rivers of Amazonia rests during the day, usually "standing" head down in its shelters. At night the fish hunt in a group for fish and shrimp. From time to time these fish shed their skin cells, which is completely normal.
Compatibility: Only with fish that will not be eaten—silver dollars, large cichlids, arowanas.

375 gal

Longfin Tetra *Brycinus longipinnis*
Also: *Alestes longipinnis*
Family: African tetras, Alestiidae (see page 16).
Characteristics: 5.25 in (13 cm), male slimmer and more colorful.
Tank/Water: 60 × 20 × 20 in (150 × 50 × 50 cm), water types 2–5, 76–85°F (24–29°C).
Care: At least six specimens in a brightly lit tank with open swimming space. Highly nutritious live and frozen foods (mosquito larvae, insects), also dry food. Water movement.
Habits: Lively schooling fish found in rain forest streams in West Africa. Lives mainly on insects that fly by.
Compatibility: Cichlids of West and Central Africa, killifish, and naked catfish.

100 gal

Macmaster's Dwarf Cichlid *Apistogramma macmasteri*
Also: Villavicencio dwarf cichlid
Family: Cichlids, Cichlidae (see page 10).
Characteristics: 2.75 in (7 cm), male larger and more colorful.
Tank/Water: 40 × 16 × 16 in (100 × 40 × 40 cm), water types 2–3, 74–79°F (23–26°C).
Care: Dark tanks that are densely planted in parts, with sand or fine gravel substrate and some small caves. Feed all smaller foods, especially small crustaceans. One male with several females.
Habits: In black water near shallow, sandy banks of rivers with leaf and wood deposits. Harem-forming cavity brooder.
Compatibility: With South American surface-dwelling characins and cichlids, such as angelfish.

37.5 gal

Madagascar Rainbowfish *Bedotia geayi*
Family: Madagascar rainbowfish, Bedotiidae (see page 18).
Characteristics: 6 in (15 cm), male larger and more colorful.
The beautiful colors are seen only in strong light.
Tank/Water: 60 × 20 × 20 in (150 × 50 × 50 cm), water types
4–6, 72–76°F (21–24°C).
Care: Schooling fish for large, brightly lit tanks, loosely planted
only along the sides, with rocky substrate in parts and good
water movement. Feed plant foods, as well as highly nutritious
frozen and live foods.
Habits: Nimble swimmer that lives in small schools in the
clear hill streams of Madagascar.
Compatibility: With all medium-sized fish of the bottom
region.

100 gal

Mahogany Characin *Neolebias ansorgii*
Also: Ansorge's characin
Family: Moonfish, Citharinidae (see page 16).
Characteristics: 1.4 in (3.5 cm), female paler and plumper.
Tank/Water: 24 × 12 × 12 in (60 × 30 × 30 cm), water types
1–2, 72–77°F (22–25°C).
Care: A few males with several females in dark tanks. Hiding
places near the bottom for the males, which defend small terri-
tories. Lightly planted. Feed fine live and frozen foods (such as
Artemia) and dry food containing plant matter.
Habits: Group fish that lives in tangled vegetation in clear run-
ning and swampy waters in Nigeria and Cameroon.
Compatibility: Only with small, placid fish such as killifish
and Aplocheilinae. No dwarf cichlids!

12.5 gal

Malawi Blue Dolphin *Cyrtocara moorii*
Family: Cichlids, Cichlidae (see page 10).
Characteristics: 8 in (20 cm), male more intense blue.
Tank/Water: 80 × 24 × 24 in (200 × 60 × 60 cm), water types
5–6, 77–81°F (25–27°C).
Care: One or many males with several females in tanks with
plenty of open swimming space over sandy areas with some
rocks in the tank background. Feed all standard foods, especially
various frozen foods (such as mature *Artemia*, mosquito larvae).
Habits: Sandy and muddy bottoms in Lake Malawi. Maternal
mouthbrooder; does not form pairs.
Compatibility: Peaceful and imposing companion fish for
Malawi tanks with species that are not rock-dwellers, such as
Copadichromis.

175 gal

Malawi Golden Cichlid *Melanochromis auratus*

Family: Cichlids, Cichlidae (see page 10).
Characteristics: 4 in (10 cm), males turn blue-black.
Tank/Water: 48 × 20 × 20 in (120 × 50 × 50 cm), water types 5–6, 77–81°F (25–27°C).

75 gal

Care: Rocks piled so that fish can swim through them. Accepts plant-based flake foods and frozen crustacean foods. Keep one or many males with several females.
Habits: Rock-dwelling Lake Malawi cichlid that occurs in a narrowly restricted area in the southern part of the lake. Eats algae, small animals, and also plankton. Maternal mouth-brooder; does not form pairs.
Compatibility: With other Lake Malawi rock cichlids, such as *Pseudotropheus* or *Metriaclima* species.

Many-banded Shell-Dweller *Neolamprologus multifasciatus*

Family: Cichlids, Cichlidae (see page 10).
Characteristics: 2 in (5 cm), female stays smaller.
Tank/Water: 24 × 12 × 12 in (60 × 30 × 30 cm), water types 5–6, 77–81°F (25–27°C).

12.5 gal

Care: Cover a sand layer about 2 in (5 cm) deep with many empty snail shells. Bring in several specimens as the foundation of a colony. Feed small crustaceans and dry foods.
Habits: Lives in colonies with often hundreds of others in large deposits of empty snail shells in Lake Tanganyika. Harem-forming cavity brooder.
Compatibility: In larger tanks with Lake Tanganyikan cichlids that do not inhabit the sand zone.

Marakely *Paratilapia bleekeri*

Also: Black diamond cichlid
Family: Cichlids, Cichlidae (see page 10).
Characteristics: 12 in (30 cm), adult males develop a humped forehead.
Tank/Water: 100 × 24 × 24 in (250 × 60 × 60 cm), water types 4–6, 74–83°F (23–28°C).

225 gal

Care: Keep as a group of about eight specimens in large tanks. Often aggressive if kept in small tanks and not in groups. Feed highly nutritious live and dry foods. Furnish tank with roots.
Habits: In tangles of dead wood in calm waters. Eats insects, fish, and crayfish. Pair-forming open spawner.
Compatibility: With large suckermouth armored catfish and with other large cichlids and characins.

Marbled Hatchetfish *Carnegiella strigata*

Family: Hatchetfish, Gastropelecidae (see page 16).

Characteristics: 1.5 in (4 cm), hard or virtually impossible to sex, female possibly plumper.

Tank/Water: 24 × 12 × 12 in (60 × 30 × 30 cm), water types 1–4, 79–86°F (26–30°C).

Care: Surface-dwelling group fish (keep at least six specimens); diet ideally should include insects (fruit flies, black mosquito larvae). If need be, will also eat dry food. Likes gentle water movement.

Habits: Exclusively a surface fish from standing and flowing waters (black water) of northern South America.

Compatibility: With all smaller and not overly lively fish of the middle and lower regions with similar water requirements.

12.5 gal

Masked Julie *Julidochromis transcriptus*

Family: Cichlids, Cichlidae (see page 10).

Characteristics: 2.75 in (7 cm), hard to sex.

Tank/Water: 24 × 12 × 12 in (60 × 30 × 30 cm), water types 5–6, 77–81°F (25–27°C).

Care: In aquariums furnished with stacked rocks. Feed frozen crustacean-based foods and high-quality dry foods. Don't change the aquarium décor; otherwise, the pairs easily become quarrelsome.

Habits: Rock zone of Lake Tanganyika. Eats small invertebrates. Usually a pair-forming cavity brooder.

Compatibility: In larger tanks with other cichlids from Lake Tanganyika, such as *Xenotilapia* and *Cyprichromis*.

Similar species: Golden julie, *J. ornatus*, 3 in (8 cm).

12.5 gal

Melon Barb *Puntius fasciatus*

Family: Carp and minnows, Cyprinidae (see page 16).

Characteristics: 6 in (15 cm), female plumper and less colorful. Displays beautiful colors only in optimal care conditions.

Tank/Water: 60 × 20 × 20 in (150 × 50 × 50 cm), water types 2–5, 72–79°F (22–26°C).

Care: Lively, agile schooling fish for tanks with plenty of swimming space and some shelters in the form of large-leaved plants or roots in the background. Feed all foods, with a large share of plants, such as zucchini and blanched spinach.

Habits: Probably native to streams in Peninsular India.

Compatibility: With bottom and surface fish from Southeast Asia, such as *Devario* or *Schistura* species.

Similar species: *Puntius filamentosus*, 6 in (15 cm).

100 gal

143

Mexican Cave Tetra *Astyanax mexicanus*

Also: Blind cave characin, *Anoptichthys jordani*, *Astyanax fasciatus*

Family: Tetras, Characidae (see page 16).

Characteristics: 3.5 in (9 cm), female squatter and plumper. Blind because of regressed eyes, and unpigmented.

Tank/Water: 32 × 14 × 16 in (80 × 35 × 40 cm), water types 4–6, 68–77°F (20–25°C).

25 gal

Care: Open swimming space for these tireless swimmers; otherwise, tank furnishings unimportant. Can be kept in normally lit tanks. Feeding unproblematic—all foods, including dry foods.

Habits: Omnivore from the caves of Mexico.

Compatibility: Don't keep with delicate species; but in larger tanks they are a good match for cichlids of the genus *Cryptoheros*.

Mexican Sailfin Molly *Poecilia velifera*

Family: Live-bearing toothcarp, Poeciliidae (see page 20).

Characteristics: 6 in (15 cm), male has copulatory organ.

Tank/Water: 60 × 20 × 20 in (150 × 50 × 50 cm), water types 6–7, 77–83°F (25–28°C).

100 gal

Care: As a group only in roomy, strongly lit brackish-water aquariums. Feed chiefly plant foods (such as plant-based dry foods, blanched lettuce leaves), for variety other food types, such as frozen *Cyclops* or *Artemia*.

Habits: Schooling fish found in waters near Mexican coast. Male carries dorsal fin erect to impress females.

Compatibility: Best with other brackish-water fish, such as archerfish (*Toxotes*).

Similar species: Sailfin molly, *P. latipinna*, 6 in (15 cm).

Midas Cichlid *Amphilophus citrinellus*

Also: Red devil, *Cichlasoma citrinellum*

Family: Cichlids, Cichlidae (see page 10).

Characteristics: 11 in (28 cm), male larger, often has bump on forehead.

Tank/Water: 120 × 28 × 24 in (300 × 70 × 60 cm), water types 5–6, 76–83°F (24–28°C).

300 gal

Care: As a group (at least eight specimens) in unplanted tanks with only a few structures and with sand or fine gravel substrate. Feed frozen foods and crustacean-based pellets.

Habits: Except in spawning period, found in open areas of Nicaraguan lakes. Pair-forming cavity brooder that sifts through the sand for its food.

Compatibility: With other Central American cichlids.

Mono *Monodactylus argenteus*

Family: Fingerfish, Monodactylidae (see page 12).
Characteristics: 10 in (25 cm), hard to sex.
Tank/Water: 100 × 32 × 28 in (250 × 80 × 70 cm), water type 7(!), 79–85°F (26–29°C).

350 gal

Care: Brackish-water fish that should not be kept in fresh water over the long term. Strongly lit tank with mangrove roots. Feed all standard highly nutritious foods, also shrimp and small fish.
Habits: Common, school-forming species from the Indo-Pacific mangrove belt; occasionally makes its way into fresh water in large rivers.
Compatibility: With other brackish-water fish, such as archer-fish (*Toxotes*) and sea/shark catfish (*Ariopsis*).

Moonlight Gourami *Trichogaster microlepis*

Family: Gouramis, Osphronemidae (see page 16).
Characteristics: 6 in (15 cm), female plumper.
Tank/Water: 48 × 20 × 20 in (120 × 50 × 50 cm), water types 2–6, 76–83°F (24–28°C).

75 gal

Care: Tank with no water movement and with plant life, including a cover of floating plants and several roots that divide up the open swimming area at the surface. Keep in pairs or, in large tanks, as a group. Diet of dry foods and, on occasion, live foods is adequate.
Habits: Native to shallow, slow-flowing or standing waters in Thailand and Myanmar, where the species hunts for water fleas, other small crustaceans, and insect larvae.
Compatibility: With peaceful fish that are not too territorial.

Moorii *Tropheus moorii*

Also: *Tropheus moorei*
Family: Cichlids, Cichlidae (see page 10).
Characteristics: About 5.25 in (13 cm), hard to sex.
Tank/Water: 60 × 24 × 24 in (150 × 60 × 60 cm), water types 5–6, 77–81°F (25–27°C).

137.5 g

Care: A few males with many females in strongly lit tanks. Feed only high-fiber foods, such as food mixes based on *Spirulina* algae and shrimp. Feeding these fish red mosquito larvae and a diet overly rich in protein will result in their death!
Habits: Shallow water in the rocky area of Lake Tanganyika. Algae eater. Mouthbrooder; does not form pairs.
Compatibility: Place together with *Tropheus duboisi*. Never with fish that need a low-fiber diet.

Mosquito Rasbora *Boraras brigittae*

Also: *Rasbora urophthalma brigittae, Rasbora brigittae*
Family: Carp and minnows, Cyprinidae (see page 16).
Characteristics: .75 in (2 cm), male more colorful and slimmer.
Tank/Water: 24 × 12 × 12 in (60 × 30 × 30 cm), water types 1–2, 79–85°F (26–29°C).

37.5 gal

Care: Keep as a school in densely planted tanks; otherwise, little tank décor needed. Feed fine live food (*Artemia*, small black mosquito larvae), as well as dry food of high nutritive value.
Habits: Gregarious fish native to the blackwater swamps and streams of southern Borneo.
Compatibility: Because the species is delicate, be very careful about the companions you choose; keep it only with smaller species that also like blackwater conditions, such as coolie loaches.

Neon Tetra *Paracheirodon innesi*

Family: Tetras, Characidae (see page 16).
Characteristics: 1.5 in (4 cm), female plumper.
Tank/Water: 24 × 12 × 12 in (60 × 30 × 30 cm), water types 1–5, 68–76°F (20–24°C).

12.5 gal

Care: Schooling fish; keep at least 15–20 specimens in tanks with subdued lighting. In imitation of the natural habitat, you can include a few brown leaves (such as red beech leaves) in the tank décor of roots and plants. Feed all small foods.
Habits: Schooling fish found in the upper reaches of small clearwater streams in the Peruvian rain forest.
Compatibility: Other small South American fish that prefer cooler temperatures.

Nicaraguan Cichlid *Hypsophrys nicaraguense*

Also: *Cichlasoma nicaraguense, Copora nicaraguense*
Family: Cichlids, Cichlidae (see page 10).
Characteristics: 10 in (25 cm), female much smaller.
Tank/Water: 60 × 24 × 24 in (150 × 60 × 60 cm), water types 5–6, 76–81°F (24–27°C).

137.5 g

Care: Keep in pairs in spacious tanks with sand or gravel substrate, a large cave, and other places to hide. Eats all standard foods.
Habits: Found in the intermediate zone between sand and rocks, usually in Nicaraguan and Costa Rican lakes. Juveniles eat insect larvae; adults also eat plants. Pair-forming cavity brooder.
Compatibility: With other Central American cichlids.

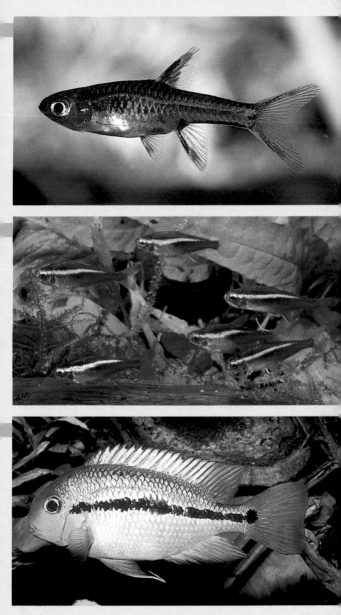

Nichols' Mouthbrooder *Pseudocrenilabrus nicholsi*
Also: *Pseudocrenilabrus ventralis*
Family: Cichlids, Cichlidae (see page 10).
Characteristics: 3 in (8 cm), female smaller, less colorful.
Tank/Water: 32 × 14 × 16 in (80 × 35 × 40 cm), water types 2–5, 76–81°F (24–27°C).
Care: One male with several females in tanks that are densely planted in parts. Varied diet of small crustaceans (*Artemia*, *Cyclops*) and dry food.
Habits: Inhabits quiet stretches of rivers and streams, often overgrown with bank vegetation, in the Upper Congo. Maternal mouthbrooder; does not form pairs.
Compatibility: With African characins (such as Congo tetras) and cichlids (such as *Nanochromis*).

25 gal

Nigerian Red Taeniatus *Pelvicachromis taeniatus*
Family: Cichlids, Cichlidae (see page 10).
Characteristics: 3 in (8 cm), female has more brilliant colors.
Tank/Water: 24 × 12 × 12 in (60 × 30 × 30 cm), water types 2–4 (depending on color form: the "Moliwe" and "Muyuka" color forms, unlike the others, dislike acid water values), 76–81°F (24–27°C).
Care: Keep in pairs in planted tanks with some water movement. Accepts all standard foods.
Habits: Found in clear rain forest streams with sandy bottom, usually overgrown with water lilies. Female's abdomen brighter when in spawning dress. Pair-former cavity brooder.
Compatibility: Good with lampeyes.
Similar species: *Pelvicachromis subocellatus*, 3.5 in (9 cm).

12.5 gal

Oaxacan Blue-Eye *Priapella intermedia*
Family: Live-bearing toothcarp, Poeciliidae (see page 20).
Characteristics: 2.75 in (7 cm), male has copulatory organ.
Tank/Water: 40 × 16 × 16 in (100 × 40 × 40 cm), water types 5–6, 77–83°F (25–28°C).
Care: Tank with good water movement, as well as adequate swimming space and loose plantings along the sides. Feed highly nutritious dry food, black mosquito larvae, and small insects. Good water maintenance especially important. Cover tank tightly, as this fish loves to leap.
Habits: Nervous schooling fish that hunts insects near the surface of fast-flowing waters in Mexico.
Compatibility: Ideal companion for small Central American cichlids, such as *Archocentrus* species.

37.5 gal

Ocellated Lamprologus *Lamprologus ocellatus*
Family: Cichlids, Cichlidae (see page 10).
Characteristics: 2.4 in (6 cm), males grow distinctly larger.
Tank/Water: 24 × 12 × 12 in (60 × 30 × 30 cm), water types 5–6, 77–81°F (25–27°C).
Care: As tank furnishings, a sand layer about 2.4 in (6 cm) deep and a sterilized snail shell for each fish are sufficient. Keep one male with one (or more, in large tanks) female. Takes all standard foods, especially small crustaceans.
Habits: Found in Lake Tanganyika, where empty snail shells lie in the sand. The males live in their own shell houses and bury others for passing females. Harem-forming cavity brooder.
Compatibility: In large tanks with *Cyprichromis*.

12.5 gal

Odessa Barb *Puntius sp.*
Also: Incorrectly, *P. ticto*
Family: Carp and minnows, Cyprinidae (see page 16).
Characteristics: 2.75 in (7 cm), male more colorful, female plumper.
Tank/Water: 40 × 16 × 16 in (100 × 40 × 40 cm), water types 2–6, 72–77°F (22–25°C).
Care: Splendid schooling fish for tanks with low water movement, loose plantings of *Cryptocoryne*, and partly sand, partly gravel substrate. Feed standard foods and plant foods.
Habits: This gregarious, lively species is probably native to Myanmar (Burma). Exact origin remains unknown; probably a stream fish.
Compatibility: With fish such as loaches and danios.

37.5 gal

Orange Bushfish *Microctenopoma ansorgii*
Also: *Ctenopoma ansorgii*
Family: Labyrinthfish, Anabantidae (see page 16).
Characteristics: 2.75 in (7 cm), male has white-edged fins.
Tank/Water: 24 × 12 × 12 in (60 × 30 × 30 cm), water types 2–4, 74–81°F (23–27°C).
Care: In pairs in densely planted, dark aquariums with many hiding places. Cover of floating plants. Feed insect larvae and other live foods.
Habits: This species lives hidden in often weed-filled stretches of smaller bodies of flowing water in the Congo basin. Males are territorial.
Compatibility: Nimble African barbs and lampeyes. In larger tanks, also with dwarf cichlids (such as *Nanochromis*).

12.5 gal

Orange Chromide *Etropius maculatus*

Family: Cichlids, Cichlidae (see page 10).

Characteristics: 3 in (8 cm), hard to sex.

Tank/Water: 32 × 14 × 16 in (80 × 35 × 40 cm), water types 6–7, 79–85°F (26–29°C).

25 gal

Care: Easy-to-keep fish; keep in pairs in tanks with sand or fine gravel substrate, hardy aquatic plants (such as *Vallisneria*), pebbles. Takes all standard foods. The species is susceptible in tanks with soft water.

Habits: Shallow bank areas of standing water bodies, often also in brackish water, in South India and Sri Lanka. Pair-forming open spawner. Occasionally the females grow larger than the males.

Compatibility: With brackish-water fish from Asia.

Orange Pike Cichlid *Crenicichla sp. "Xingu 1"*

Family: Cichlids, Cichlidae (see page 10).

Characteristics: 16 in (40 cm), adult female has red belly. Only juveniles have typical striped pattern.

Tank/Water: 128 × 24 × 24 in (320 × 60 × 60 cm), water types 2–4, 81–86°F (27–30°C).

300 gal

Care: Raise school of fry, and after pair formation, give away the surplus specimens. Feed live fish or fish meat. If aggressions develop within a pair, separate them with a pane of glass in the aquarium. Tanks with roots, stone slabs, and strong water movement.

Habits: Predator that lives in the rocky areas of the Rio Xingu, a clearwater river in Amazonia. Pair-forming cavity brooder.

Compatibility: Large suckermouth armored catfish and cichlids.

Orange-tailed Goodeid *Xenotoca eiseni*

Also: Red-tailed goodeid

Family: Splitfins, Goodeidae (see page 20).

Characteristics: About 2.75 in (7 cm), male much more colorful.

Tank/Water: 24 × 12 × 12 in (60 × 30 × 30 cm), water types 4–6; 65–79°F (18–26°C).

12.5 gal

Care: If fed enough plant foods (such as blanched lettuce leaves), a peaceful and undemanding group fish for planted tanks. Occasionally feed small crustaceans and dry foods as well.

Habits: Group fish native to moderately flowing streams and rivers in the highlands of Mexico.

Compatibility: With other live-bearers and small Central American cichlids. Long-finned fish may be bothered by "fin-nibbling."

Orinoco Piranha *Pygocentrus notatus*

Also: *Serrasalmus nattereri*
Family: Serrasalminae, family Characidae (see page 16).
Characteristics: 12 in (30 cm), hard to sex. Has knife-sharp teeth!
Tank/Water: 128 × 24 × 24 in (320 × 60 × 60 cm), water types 2–5, 77–83°F (25–28°C).

300 gal

Care: Raise a group of fry in large tanks with sword plants, roots, and fine gravel substrate. Feed highly nutritious diet of fish meat. Never put your bare hands into a piranha aquarium!
Habits: Schooling predator of fish in the large rivers of Venezuela. They usually hunt at dusk.
Compatibility: With large suckermouth armored catfish.
Similar species: Red piranha, *Pygocentrus nattereri*, 14 in (35 cm).

Ornate Bichir *Polypterus ornatipinnis*

Family: Bichirs, Polypteridae (see page 6).
Characteristics: 24 in (60 cm), male has larger anal fin. Juveniles' coloration richer in contrast than that of adults.
Tank/Water: 80 × 24 × 16 in (200 × 60 × 40 cm), water types 2–5, 77–83°F (25–28°C).

125 gal

Care: Often aggressive toward each other. This species is better kept singly in aquariums with a shelter (root, bamboo cane). Feed highly nutritious foods, such as fish meat, shrimp, pellets.
Habits: Predator found in large rivers of the Congo basin.
Compatibility: Only with larger fish of the Congo basin that are not regarded as food—moonfish (*Distichodus*) and naked catfish (such as *Synodontis angelicus* and *S. decorus*).

Oscar *Astronotus ocellatus*

Also: Peacock cichlid
Family: Cichlids, Cichlidae (see page 10).
Characteristics: 18 in (45 cm), hard to sex.
Tank/Water: 100 × 28 × 24 in (250 × 70 × 60 cm), water types 2–4, 77–85°F (25–29°C).

250 gal

Care: As a group in tanks furnished with roots. Ideally, do not feed pellets, but raw fish, crustaceans, insects, and occasionally green foods (fresh or in frozen form).
Habits: Widely distributed in Amazonia, in quiet waters, where it eats fish, largish insects, and crustaceans. Pair-forming open spawner.
Compatibility: With peaceful large fish, such as large suckermouth armored catfish (*Pterygoplichthys*) and large *Crenicichla*.

Panamanian Yellow Cichlid *Archocentrus nanoluteus*

Family: Cichlids, Cichlidae (see page 10).

Characteristics: 4 in (10 cm), females stay somewhat smaller.

Tank/Water: 40 × 16 × 16 in (100 × 40 × 40 cm), water types 5–6, 76–83°F (24–28°C).

Care: Very peaceful species; keep in pairs in tanks loosely planted with large-leaved plants and with a rock cave and fine gravel substrate. Feed all standard foods.

Habits: Known to be native only to a small river system in Panama. Pair-forming cavity brooder.

Compatibility: With a group of live-bearing toothcarp that enjoy swimming, such as black-bellied limias.

Similar species: *Archocentrus altoflavus,* 4 in (10 cm).

37.5 gal

Panda Cory *Corydoras panda*

Family: Callichthyid armored catfish, Callichthyidae (see page 9).

Characteristics: 2 in (5 cm), female plumper.

Tank/Water: 24 × 12 × 12 in (60 × 30 × 30 cm), water types 2–6, 74–79°F (23–26°C).

Care: Keep as a group in tanks with sandy substrate in parts, loose plantings, and structures where the fish can go to rest. Feed fine live, frozen, and dry foods. Especially fond of frozen *Cyclops* and moderate temperatures.

Habits: Gregarious fish found in sandy stretches of medium-sized rivers of the Peruvian Amazon.

Compatibility: Ideal tankmate for South American fish of the middle and upper tank regions. In small tanks, not with cichlids.

12.5 gal

Panda Dwarf Cichlid *Apistogramma nijsseni*

Family: Cichlids, Cichlidae (see page 10).

Characteristics: 3.5 in (9 cm), male larger and more colorful.

Tank/Water: 40 × 16 × 16 in (100 × 40 × 40 cm), water types 1–3, 76–81°F (24–27°C).

Care: In dark, blackwater tanks with roots, loose plantings, and some small caves. Feed all standard foods. Feed small crustaceans to promote red coloration.

Habits: In the shallow-water/leaf-litter stratum of sandy blackwater streams in the Peruvian Amazon. Pair-forming cavity brooder. Probably eats insect larvae.

Compatibility: With peaceful cichlids of the middle tank region, such as angelfish, and with characins.

Similar species: Blue panda apisto, *A. panduro,* 3.5 in (9 cm).

37.5 gal

Paradise Fish *Macropodus opercularis*

Family: Paradise fish, family Osphronemidae (see page 16).
Characteristics: 4 in (10 cm), male longer finned, more colorful.
Tank/Water: 32 × 14 × 16 in (80 × 35 × 40 cm), water types 2–6, 68–79°F (20–26°C).
Care: Keep in pairs in tanks with many structures, floating plants, loose plantings, and roots. Feed all standard foods.
Habits: Swampy areas, canals, and quiet stretches of rivers in Vietnam and southern China. Territorial.
Compatibility: With medium-sized Asian barbs, such as the Odessa barb, and loaches, such as *Botia* species. Can get rough with shy fish.
Similar species: Black paradise fish, *M. spechti*, 5 in (12 cm).

25 gal

Parrot platy *Xiphophorus variatus var.*

Family: Live-bearing toothcarp, Poeciliidae (see page 20).
Characteristics: 2.75 in (7 cm), male has copulatory organ.
Tank/Water: 32 × 14 × 16 in (80 × 35 × 40 cm), water types 4–6, 72–77°F (22–25°C).
Care: Group fish for loosely planted tanks. All smaller foods. Don't forget plant foods!
Habits: The wild form lives in groups in lowland waters of Central America with moderate current. There it eats chiefly algae deposits.
Compatibility: Undemanding fish for a community tank with all not overly large fish species with similar water requirements.
Similar species: There are a great many cultivated forms, some of which, such as the marigold platy, may be sensitive.

25 gal

Peaceful Betta *Betta imbellis*

Also: Small fighter, *Betta rubra*
Family: Fighting fish of the family Osphronemidae (see page 16).
Characteristics: 2 in (5 cm), female pale, with shorter fins.
Tank/Water: 24 × 12 × 12 in (60 × 30 × 30 cm), water types 2–5, 79–83°F (26–28°C).
Care: In small tanks in pairs; in larger tanks at least 32 in (80 cm) long, keep several pairs. Dense plantings and lots of structures create territorial boundaries and places to hide. Feed small live, frozen, and dry foods. Floating-plant cover.
Habits: Swampy regions of eastern Thailand and Malaysia.
Compatibility: Small peaceful fish of the lower and middle tank regions: small barbs or danios and rasboras (such as *Boraras*) and loaches, such as *Pangio kuhlii*.

12.5 gal

Peacock Goby *Tateurndina ocellicauda*

Also: Eye-spot goby
Family: Sleeper gobies, Eleotridae (see page 11).
Characteristics: 2 in (5 cm), female plumper, with shorter fins.
Tank/Water: 24 × 12 × 12 in (60 × 30 × 30 cm), water types 2–5, 79–85°F (26–29°C).
Care: In well-planted tanks with several caves, keep one or two males with several females. Feed fine live and dry foods. No water movement.
Habits: Native to clear, gently flowing waters in New Guinea.
Compatibility: With small fish from New Guinea, such as filament rainbows or spotted blue-eyes.
Similar species: True gobies, *Hypseleotris cf. compressiceps,* 2.75 in (7 cm); *Hemieleotris latifasciatus,* 3 in (8 cm).

12.5 gal

Pearl Danio *Danio albolineatus*

Also: *Brachydanio albolineatus*
Family: Carp and minnows, Cyprinidae (see page 16).
Characteristics: 2.2 in (5.5 cm), female plumper.
Tank/Water: 32 × 14 × 16 in (80 × 35 × 40 cm), water types 2–6, 72–79°F (22–26°C).
Care: In tanks with water movement, pebbles, and moderately bright lighting that shows the iridescent colors to good effect. Takes all standard foods.
Habits: Agile surface dweller in fast-flowing streams of Southeast Asia, where it hunts for insects.
Compatibility: Ideal with bottom-dwelling Asian stream fish, such as stream loaches (*Schistura, Nemacheilus*) or *Gastromyzon.*
Similar species: Kerr's danio, *Danio kerri,* 2 in (5 cm).

25 gal

Pearl Gourami *Trichogaster leerii*

Family: Gouramis, Osphronemidae (see page 16).
Characteristics: 5 in (12 cm), male has orange-red chest.
Tank/Water: 40 × 16 × 16 in (100 × 40 × 40 cm), water types 2–4, 77–85°F (25–29°C).
Care: Dark tanks with cover of floating plants and plenty of structures in the form of roots. Feed various live, frozen, and dry foods. Peat filtration recommended. No water movement.
Habits: Group fish found in shallow zones of warm, quiet stretches of Indonesian rivers and lakes. Often in black water. Males aggressive in spawning season.
Compatibility: With other blackwater fish of Southeast Asia, such as barbs (fiveband barbs), danios, and rasboras (red-striped rasbora), and loaches (coolie loaches).

37.5 gal

Penguin Fish *Thayeria boehlkei*

Family: Tetras, Characidae (see page 16).
Characteristics: Up to about 2 in (5 cm), female plumper.
Tank/Water: 32 × 14 × 16 in (80 × 35 × 40 cm), water types 2–5, 76–83°F (24–28°C).

25 gal

Care: At least six to eight specimens in loosely planted tanks, where they inhabit the middle to upper tank strata. Feed all smaller foods, especially mosquito larvae and small insects.
Habits: Schooling fish native to South America.
Compatibility: Peaceful species, a good match for tetras that live closer to the bottom (*Hemigrammus, Hyphessobrycon*), dwarf cichlids (*Apistogramma, Laetacara*), callichthyid armored catfish (*Corydoras*), and whiptail catfish (*Rineloricaria*).
Similar species: *Thayeria obliqua*, 3 in (8 cm).

Peppered Catfish *Corydoras paleatus*

Family: Callichthyid catfish, Callichthyidae (see page 9).
Characteristics: 2.75 in (7 cm), female plumper.
Tank/Water: 32 × 14 × 16 in (80 × 35 × 40 cm), water types 2–6, 65–74°F (18–23°C).

25 gal

Care: Keep as a group in tanks with sandy substrate in parts, loose plantings, and structures where the fish can go to rest. Feed fine live, frozen, and dry foods. Especially prizes frozen *Cyclops* and moderate temperatures.
Habits: Gregarious fish from sandy stretches of medium-sized rivers of La Plata basin in South America.
Compatibility: Ideal companion for South American fish of the middle and upper tank regions that are not too fond of warmth.

Peter's Elephant Nose *Gnathonemus petersii*

Family: Elephant noses, Mormyridae (see page 7).
Characteristics: 14 in (35 cm), male has concave anal fin.
Tank/Water: 48 × 20 × 20 in (120 × 50 × 50 cm) (for single specimen), for group, tank at least 80 in (200 cm) long. Water types 2–5, 76–83°F (24–28°C).

75 gal

Care: Singly in smaller tanks or as a group in larger tanks. Each fish needs its own hiding place in dark tanks. In the evening feed live worms and red mosquito larvae.
Habits: Predominantly nocturnal fish from soft-bottomed river courses in Central Africa. Uses electric signals for communication and orientation. Often aggressive toward each other.
Compatibility: Only with small fish that will not eat the elephant noses' food. No cichlids!

Phuket Loach *Schistura robertsi*

Family: Loaches of the family Balitoridae (see page 17).

Characteristics: 2.75 in (7 cm), hard to sex.

Tank/Water: 32 × 14 × 16 in (80 × 35 × 40 cm), water types 3–6, 74–79°F (23–26°C).

Care: Like most other *Schistura*, it likes good water movement and a tank furnished with pebbles and hiding places. Keep singly or as a group of at least six specimens. Feed live, frozen, and dry foods.

Habits: Stream fish found in rain forest streams on the Thai vacation island of Phuket and the nearby mainland. Probably eats mainly insect larvae hidden in the streambed.

Compatibility: Small rasboras and danios, such as *Danio* species.

25 gal

Platinum Hatchetfish *Thoracharax securis*

Family: Hatchetfish, Gasteropelecidae (see page 16).

Characteristics: 3.5 in (9 cm), female probably plumper.

Tank/Water: 48 × 24 × 20 in (120 × 60 × 50 cm), water types 2–4, 77–86°F (25–30°C).

Care: As a school in roomy aquariums, with the water level somewhat lowered so as to create a 4-in (10-cm) wide space between the water surface and the cover pane. A few floating plants. Feed insects (such as fruit flies) and black mosquito larvae.

Habits: Insect-eating surface fish found in large rivers in Amazonia; thanks to its powerful chest muscles it can "fly" several feet across the water.

Compatibility: With peaceful medium-sized cichlids (angelfish, discus, triangle cichlids).

87.5 gal

Platy *Xiphophorus maculatus var.*

Family: Livebearing toothcarps, Poeciliidae (see page 20).

Characteristics: 2.4 in (6 cm), male has copulatory organ.

Tank/Water: 24 × 12 × 12 in (60 × 30 × 30 cm), water types 4–6, 70–77°F (21–25°C).

Care: Lively group fish for loosely planted tanks. All smaller foods. Plant foods.

Habits: The wild form lives in groups in flowing lowland waters of Central America, where it eats chiefly algae and animals found in the algae.

Compatibility: Can share a tank with all fish species that are not overly large and have similar water requirements.

Similar species: There are a great many cultivated forms, some of which can be sensitive.

12.5 gal

Powder Blue Cichlid *Pseudotropheus socolofi*
Also: *Pseudotropheus sp. "pindani"*
Family: Cichlids, Cichlidae (see page 10).
Characteristics: 5 in (12 cm), hard to sex.
Tank/Water: 60 × 20 × 20 in (150 × 50 × 50 cm), water types 5–6, 77–81°F (25–27°C).

87.5 gal

Care: Keep one or many males with several females. Pile up rock clusters so that fish can swim through them. Feed plant-based dry foods and small crustaceans (live or frozen).
Habits: Algae and plankton eater found in the rock zone of Lake Malawi. Like almost all other Malawi cichlids, a maternal mouthbrooder that does not form pairs.
Compatibility: With other Lake Malawi cichlids, such as *Pseudotropheus* or *Metriaclima* species.

Quetzal Cichlid *Vieja synspila*
Also: *Cichlasoma synspilum*
Family: Cichlids, Cichlidae (see page 10).
Characteristics: 14 in (35 cm), males grow bigger, develop more brilliant colors, and have a large forehead bump.
Tank/Water: 100 × 28 × 28 in (250 × 70 × 70 cm), water types 5–6, 76–83°F (24–28°C).

300 gal

Care: In a group or in pairs in loosely structured tanks with lots of room in the foreground and hiding places (roots, rock slabs) in the background. Eats various plant foods.
Habits: Primarily herbivorous fish found in slow-flowing waters, cloudy in parts, in Central America. Pair-forming open spawner.
Compatibility: Peaceful large cichlids from Central America.

Rainbow Snakehead *Channa bleheri*
Also: Jewel snakehead
Family: Snakeheads, Channidae (see page 15).
Characteristics: 6 in (15 cm), female smaller and plumper.
Tank/Water: 40 × 16 × 16 in (100 × 40 × 40 cm), water types 3–6, 74–77°F (23–25°C).

25 gal

Care: Keep in pairs in loosely planted tanks. Each fish needs its own hiding place in the form of a roomy cave. This shy species should be fed various highly nutritious frozen foods, insects, small pieces of fish, and rainworms.
Habits: Occurs in streams in northeastern India, where the species probably eats insects and occasionally small fish.
Compatibility: Best kept in a species tank.
Similar species: *Channa orientalis*, 6 in (15 cm).

Ram Cichlid *Mikrogeophagus ramirezi*
Also: *Papiliochromis ramirezi*
Family: Cichlids, Cichlidae (see page 10).
Characteristics: 2 in (5 cm), female has crimson belly, male has elongated dorsal fin membranes.
Tank/Water: 24 × 12 × 12 in (60 × 30 × 30 cm), water types 1–3, 79–86°F (26–30°C).
Care: If the water values are right, an unproblematic fish; keep in pairs in tanks that are densely planted in parts. All smaller foods.
Habits: Found in quiet, plant-rich savannah waters in Venezuela/Colombia. Pair-forming open spawner.
Compatibility: In somewhat larger tanks, with characins that live near the surface and with cavity-brooding dwarf cichlids.

12.5 gal

Red Flag Cichlid *Laetacara dorsigera*
Also: *Aequidens dorsiger*
Family: Cichlids, Cichlidae (see page 10).
Characteristics: 2.75 in (7 cm), hard to sex.
Tank/Water: 24 × 12 × 12 in (60 × 30 × 30 cm), water types 2–4, 79–86°F (26–30°C).
Care: In pairs in tanks that are densely planted in parts and include a few lime-free pebbles. Feed mainly fine live foods, as well as dry foods.
Habits: Plant-rich, low-current waters in the area where Bolivia, Argentina, and Brazil meet. Pair-forming open spawner.
Compatibility: Peaceful species suitable for community aquariums with calm characins and other calm fish, such as angelfish or discus.

12.5 gal

Red Phantom Tetra *Hyphessobrycon sweglesi*
Also: *Megalomphodus sweglesi*
Family: Tetras, Characidae (see page 16).
Characteristics: 1.5 in (4 cm), male more intense red.
Tank/Water: 24 × 12 × 12 in (60 × 30 × 30 cm), water types 2–4, 72–79°F (22–26°C).
Care: Peaceful schooling fish for dark tanks that are not too warm and are densely planted in parts. Takes all smaller foods.
Habits: Like most other *Hyphessobrycon* species, *H. sweglesi* males temporarily establish small mating territories that they defend against other males of the species. Origin: Orinoco River system in Colombia.
Compatibility: With small South American fish, such as callichthyid armored catfish and dwarf cichlids.

12.5 gal

Red-finned Lampeye *Procatopus nototaenia*

Family: Lampeyes, family Poeciliidae (see page 20).

Characteristics: 2 in (5 cm), male more colorful, bigger fins.

Tank/Water: 40 × 16 × 16 in (100 × 40 × 40 cm), water types 2–5, 72–77°F (22–25°C).

Care: Partially dark tanks with good water movement and some roots or stones. Feed small insects, black mosquito larvae, and dry foods.

37.5 gal

Habits: Lively, current-loving schooling fish found in clear, flowing waters of the rain forest in Cameroon's hill country. Hunts for insects and other food in the current.

Compatibility: Ideal companion fish for West and Central African dwarf cichlids (*Pelvicachromis, Nanochromis*), killifish (*Epiplatys*), and barbs.

Red-finned Suckermouth Catfish
Parotocinclus maculicauda

Family: Suckermouth armored catfish, Loricariidae (see page 9).

Characteristics: 2 in (5 cm), male has red-tipped fins.

Tank/Water: 24 × 12 × 12 in (60 × 30 × 30 cm), water types 3–6, 68–77°F (20–25°C).

12.5 gal

Care: Gregarious species that should be kept in a small group (five or six specimens). Furnish tanks with large-leaved plants, roots, and pebbles. Be sure to maintain good water quality (regular water change is absolutely essential). Takes small frozen foods (such as *Artemia, Cyclops*), as well as green foods (such as blanched spinach leaves) or green food tablets.

Habits: Native to streams in southwestern Brazil.

Compatibility: With all small characins, cichlids, and catfish.

Redhook Silver Dollar *Myleus rubripinnis*

Family: Serrasalminae, family Characidae (see page 16).

Characteristics: 16 in (40 cm), adult female is plumper.

Tank/Water: 128 × 28 × 28 in (320 × 70 × 70 cm), water types 2–5, 77–83°F (25–28°C).

350 gal

Care: Striking characin for large, unplanted tanks that offer open swimming space on the one hand, and roots as shelters to rest in on the other hand. Feed green foods and plant-based dry foods. Timid species—only for aquariums in a quiet spot.

Habits: School-forming large characin (keep at least six specimens) found in large South American rivers, where it eats leaves from overhanging trees along the river banks.

Compatibility: In large tanks with peaceful large cichlids (such as *Geophagus*) and catfish (such as *Sorubim*).

Red-striped Rasbora *Rasbora pauciperforata*
Also: Red-lined rasbora
Family: Carp and minnows, Cyprinidae (see page 16).
Characteristics: About 2.75 in (7 cm), female plumper.
Tank/Water: 32 × 14 × 16 in (80 × 35 × 40 cm), water types 1–4, 77–83°F (25–28°C).
Care: Keep a small school with at least six specimens in dark tanks with peat filtration. Loose plantings or finely branched roots. Takes all smaller foods, also dry foods.
Habits: Schooling fish that tends to live near the surface of black water in Southeast Asia (Malaysia, Indonesia).
Compatibility: With labyrinthfish that have similar needs (such as gouramis), loaches (such as *Botia* species), and rasboras (such as harlequin rasboras).

25 gal

Redtail Notho *Nothobranchius guentheri*
Family: Killifish, Aplocheilidae (see page 19).
Characteristics: 2.4 in (6 cm), male bigger and more colorful.
Tank/Water: 24 × 12 × 12 in (60 × 30 × 30 cm), water types 5–6, 74–76°F (23–24°C).
Care: In a 74-in (60-cm) tank (about three males with three to six females). Dense plantings in parts, dim lighting, dark substrate. Feed live (including tubifex), frozen, and occasionally dry foods.
Habits: Omnivore found on the Tanzanian island of Zanzibar in marshy savannah pools and streams that dry up in the dry season.
Compatibility: Best kept in a single-species aquarium.
Similar species: *Nothobranchius rachovii*, 2.4 in (6 cm).

12.5 gal

Red-tailed Black Shark *Epalzeorhynchus bicolor*
Also: *Labeo bicolor*
Family: Carp and minnows, Cyprinidae (see page 16).
Characteristics: 6 in (15 cm), adult males thinner.
Tank/Water: 48 × 20 × 20 in (120 × 50 × 50 cm), water types 2–6, 74–83°F (23–28°C).
Care: Territory-forming species. To keep several, only very large tanks are suitable—dark tanks with shelter, consisting of roots, for example. Eats all smaller foods, especially green foods.
Habits: Using its downward-facing mouth, it grazes on rocks and roots in larger flowing waters of Thailand.
Compatibility: Because of its aggressiveness, keep only with fish that are nimble or fit to fight, such as larger barbs.
Similar species: Red-finned shark, *E. cf. frenatus*, 5 in (12 cm).

75 gal

Reedfish *Erpetoichthys calabaricus*
Also: *Calamoichthys calabaricus*
Family: Bichirs, Polypteridae (see page 6).
Characteristics: 14.5 in (37 cm), male has larger anal fin.
Length often wrongly stated as 35 in (90 cm).
Tank/Water: 32 × 16 × 16 in (80 × 40 × 40 cm), water types
2–5, 79–85°F (26–29°C).
Care: Gregarious fish for densely planted tanks with lots of
hiding places and with no water movement. Feed frozen foods
(adult *Artemia*, shrimp, insects). Some refuse to eat; watch
them being fed before you buy!
Habits: Swamp dweller whose range extends from the coastal
lowlands of Nigeria to the Congo. Eats mainly shrimp.
Compatibility: With larger West African fish.

30 gal

Rock Krib *Paralabidochromis sp. "rock kribensis"*
Also: *"Haplochromis" sp. "rock-kribensis"*
Family: Cichlids, Cichlidae (see page 10).
Characteristics: 5 in (12 cm), male colorful and larger.
Tank/Water: 48 × 20 × 20 in (120 × 50 × 50 cm), water types
4–6, 76–81°F (24–27°C).
Care: One or many males with several females in loosely struc-
tured tanks (rocks, large-leaved plants). Feed crustacean-based
foods (such as *Cyclops*), frozen mosquito larvae, and dry foods.
Habits: Rock dweller native to Lake Victoria, where the species
picks insect larvae and other foods out of cracks in rocks.
Compatibility: Other Lake Victoria cichlids.
Similar species: *Pundamilia nyererei*, 5 in (12 cm).

75 gal

Rosy Barb *Puntius conchonius*
Family: Carp and minnows, Cyprinidae (see page 16).
Characteristics: 5 in (12 cm), male red, female silvery olive
green.
Tank/Water: 48 × 20 × 20 in (120 × 50 × 50 cm), water types
2–6, 61–72°F (16–22°C).
Care: Large aquariums with lots of swimming space for this
group fish. Tender plants will be eaten. Best placed in garden
pond in summer and fished out in fall. Feed foods containing
plant matter, as well as insect larvae.
Habits: Lively inhabitant of streams and lakes in northern
India and neighboring areas; loves cooler water.
Compatibility: With all bottom or surface fish that tolerate
cooler water, such as hillstream loaches or paradise fish.

75 gal

Rosy Tetra *Hyphessobrycon rosaceus*

Also: *Hyphessobrycon bentosi*
Family: Tetras, Characidae (see page 16).
Characteristics: 1.75 in (4.5 cm), males longer-finned.
Tank/Water: 24 × 12 × 12 in (60 × 30 × 30 cm), water types 2–5, 74–81°F (23–27°C).

12.5 gal

Care: Good group fish for bright and loosely planted community tanks. Slight water movement promotes liveliness. All food.
Habits: Lively group fish that swims in the gentle current of sandy or gravelly streams.
Compatibility: In larger tanks, with dwarf cichlids (such as *Apistogramma, Nannacara*); otherwise with callichthyid armored catfish, other tetras, and smaller suckermouth armored catfish (such as *Rineloricaria*).

Royal Farlowella *Sturisoma festivum*

Also: Golden whiptail, *Sturisoma aureum, S. panamense*
Family: Suckermouth armored catfish, Loricariidae (see page 9).
Characteristics: 10 in (25 cm), male has whiskers.
Tank/Water: 48 × 20 × 20 in (120 × 50 × 50 cm), water types 2–5, 77–85°F (25–29°C).

75 gal

Care: Horizontally placed root branches in dark tanks, with half the tank an open sandy surface. Feed green foods, food tablets, frozen small crustaceans.
Habits: In tangles of submerged wood in quiet-flowing waters of the Amazon basin.
Compatibility: Good companion fish for peaceful dwarf and large cichlids from South America, but characins as well.
Similar species: *Sturisomatichthys leightoni,* about 6 in (15 cm).

Royal Pleco *Panaque nigrolineatus*

Family: Suckermouth armored catfish, Loricariidae (see page 9).
Characteristics: 22 in (55 cm), in spawning season male has long spines (odontodes) near the gill covers.
Tank/Water: 128 × 32 × 28 in (320 × 80 × 70 cm), water types 2–5, 77–85°F (25–29°C).

450 gal

Care: Most important, besides a spacious aquarium, is the presence of many roots or other pieces of wood, which these catfish will quickly chew on and completely consume. Wood is essential for proper care of this beautiful species. Roomy caves and additional green foods (such as cabbage leaves). Heavy filtration to deal with their copious amounts of waste.
Habits: Wood eater found in rivers of the Amazon basin.
Compatibility: Peaceful, even with small fish.

Rummy-Nose Tetra *Hemigrammus bleheri*
Family: Tetras, Characidae (see page 16).
Characteristics: 1.75 in (4.5 cm), female plumper.
Tank/Water: 32 × 14 × 16 in (80 × 35 × 40 cm), water types 1–3, 72–79°F (22–26°C).
Care: Long-lived aquarium fish if proper water values are maintained and if kept in a school (at least 10 specimens). Best for loosely planted, dark tanks with low water movement. Feed all standard small foods.
Habits: Decidedly lively schooling fish native to clearwater and blackwater streams of the Rio Negro in the Amazon River basin.
Compatibility: In larger tanks at least 40 in (100 cm) long, ideal community fish to keep with dwarf cichlids and discus fish.
Similar species: *Hemigrammus rhodostomus*, 2 in (5 cm).

37.5 gal

Sailfin Pleco *Glyptoperichthys gibbiceps*
Also: Leopard pleco, *Pterogoplichthys gibbiceps*
Family: Suckermouth armored catfish, Loricariidae (see page 9).
Characteristics: Maximum of 20 in (50 cm), male slimmer.
Tank/Water: 128 × 28 × 28 in (320 × 70 × 70 cm), water types 2–6, 77–86°F (25–30°C).
Care: Singly or in a small group in aquariums with tubelike hiding places for each specimen. Root wood as source of fiber, green foods, pellets.
Habits: Gregarious crepuscular and diurnal species, able to survive even in hot, oxygen-poor residual water pools, thanks to its use of intestinal respiration. Native to the Amazon.
Compatibility: Peaceful species that can even be combined with small fish of all species.

375 gal

Sajica Cichlid *Archocentrus sajica*
Also: *Cichlasoma sajica*, *Cryptoheros sajica*
Family: Cichlids, Cichlidae (see page 10).
Characteristics: 4 in (10 cm), male larger, longer-finned.
Tank/Water: 40 × 16 × 16 in (100 × 40 × 40 cm), water types 5–6, 76–83°F (24–28°C).
Care: Keep in pairs in tanks furnished with roots and stones, possibly including large-leaved plants. A cave as a territorial center. Feed all standard foods.
Habits: Found in Costa Rican rivers and streams with slight current and fine gravel bottom. Primarily herbivorous. Pair-forming cavity brooder.
Compatibility: With a group of live-bearing toothcarp, such as platys or swordtails.

37.5 gal

Salt-and-Pepper Catfish *Corydoras habrosus*
Also: *Corydoras cochui*
Family: Callichthyid armored catfish, Callichthyidae (see page 9).
Characteristics: 1.2 in (3 cm), female more compact.
Tank/Water: 24 × 12 × 12 in (60 × 30 × 30 cm), water types 2–6, 76–81°F (24–27°C).

12.5 gal

Care: Can easily be kept in small tanks with sand substrate and loose plantings. Takes fine live and frozen foods, but also eats food tablets. Feed special food for *Corydoras*!
Habits: Group-forming, quite lively fish. One of the smallest callichthyid armored catfish. Known to be native only to a few stream or river courses in Venezuela.
Compatibility: Only with other small or dainty fish, such as small characins or whiptail catfish.

Sawbwa Barb *Sawbwa resplendens*
Also: Naked microrasbora
Family: Carp and minnows, Cyprinidae (see page 16).
Characteristics: 1.75 in (4.5 cm), female is colorless.
Tank/Water: 32 × 14 × 16 in (80 × 35 × 40 cm), water types 5–6, 70–76°F (21–24°C).

25 gal

Care: Keep about 15 specimens in loosely planted (for example, with *Vallisneria*, Java moss) 32-in (80-cm) tanks. Feed *Artemia* or *Cyclops* (frozen or live), occasionally dry food as well. Keep only in hard, cool water!
Habits: Schooling fish found in glass-clear, relatively cool Inle Lake in the high hills of Myanmar.
Compatibility: Keep only with bottom fish that also like cooler water, such as *Corydoras paleatus*.

Scarlet Pleco *Pseudacanthus sp. "L25"*
Family: Suckermouth armored catfish, Loricariidae (see page 9).
Characteristics: 16 in (40 cm), male has stouter spines.
Tank/Water: 100 × 32 × 28 in (250 × 80 × 70 cm), water types 2–5, 77–83°F (25–28°C).

350 gal

Care: Peaceful large catfish that needs big shelters formed by wood roots and stone slabs. Feed muscle tissue, shrimp, and green food pellets. Heavy filtration and extremely conscientious water maintenance very important, as with all loricariid catfish. Each fish/pair needs its own hiding place.
Habits: Occurs only in the clearwater river Xingu, in Brazil.
Compatibility: Good tankmate for large cichlids because of its peaceful nature, though it is well able to defend itself.
Similar species: *Pseudacanthus spinosus*, about 12 in (30 cm).

Scat *Scatophagus argus*
Also: Argus fish, spotted scat
Family: Scats, Scatophagidae (see page 13).
Characteristics: 15 in (38 cm), no known sex differences.
Tank/Water: 100 × 32 × 28 in (250 × 80 × 70 cm), water type 7, 79–85°F (26–29°C).

100 gal

Care: Gregarious species that cannot be kept in a pure freshwater aquarium over a long period. Keep as a group in large tanks with mangrove roots and lots of open swimming space. Feed all food types, including plants.
Habits: Omnivore from the brackish waters of mangrove swamps and lower reaches of rivers in the Indo-Pacific region.
Compatibility: With other mangrove fish, such as archerfish and monos.

Serpae Tetra *Hyphessobrycon eques*
Also: Jewel tetra, *Hyphessobrycon callistus*, *Hyphesso-brycon serpae*
Family: Tetras, Characidae (see page 16).
Characteristics: 1.75 in (4.5 cm), female somewhat paler.
Tank/Water: 24 × 12 × 12 in (60 × 30 × 30 cm), water types 1–5, 76–83°F (24–28°C).

12.5 gal

Care: Keep a small school with several females and males in well-planted, dark tanks with sufficient space to swim. Peat filtration recommended. Feed smaller foods.
Habits: Group fish from quiet, often vegetation-rich areas of waters in the Amazon system. Often in black water.
Compatibility: *Corydoras*, hatchetfish (such as *Carnegiella strigata*); in larger tanks, with dwarf cichlids,

Shark Catfish *Ariopsis seemanni*
Also: *Arius seemanni*
Family: Sea catfish, Ariidae (see page 9).
Characteristics: 18 in (45 cm), hard to sex.
Tank/Water: 128 × 28 × 28 in (320 × 70 × 70 cm), water types 6–7, 74–81°F (23–27°C).

125 gal

Care: Brackish-water fish that should be kept only temporarily in pure fresh water. Tank should include plenty of open swimming space and few structures. Feed highly nutritious diet of shrimp, fish. Strong filtration.
Habits: Restless swimmer found in lower reaches of large Central and South American rivers that flow into the Pacific. Fast-growing omnivore.
Compatibility: Only with brackish-water fish.

Short-nosed Clown Tetra *Distichodus sexfasciatus*

Family: Moonfish, Citharinidae (see page 16).

Characteristics: At least 10 in (25 cm); according to one report, over 20 in (50 cm). Hard to sex. The juveniles' beautiful coloration grows paler with increasing age.

Tank/Water: At least $100 \times 24 \times 24$ in ($250 \times 60 \times 60$ cm), water types 2–5, 77–83°F (25–28°C).

Care: Only in plant-free, huge aquariums that are furnished with roots. Needs large quantities of green foods and, because so much waste is produced, a substantial filtration system. Keep as a group.

Habits: Fruit and plant eater found in the large rivers of the Congo basin, also in Lake Tanganyika.

Compatibility: With large African fish.

225 gal

Siamese Algae Eater *Crossocheilus oblongus*

Also: *Crossocheilus siamensis*

Family: Carp and minnows, Cyprinidae (see page 16).

Characteristics: 6 in (15 cm), no known sexual differences.

Tank/Water: $48 \times 20 \times 20$ in ($120 \times 50 \times 50$ cm), water types 2–5, 76–83°F (24–28°C).

Care: Superb algae eater for larger aquariums; three to five specimens will eat even stubborn algae in tanks otherwise furnished with lots of structures in the form of roots and stones. Feed chiefly plant-based dry food tablets.

Habits: Bottom fish found in Southeast Asian rivers, where the species lives mainly on algae.

Compatibility: Peaceful, robust companion fish for almost all other fish, even smaller ones.

75 gal

Siamese Fighting Fish *Betta splendens*

Family: Fighting fish, Osphronemidae (see page 16).

Characteristics: 2.4 in (6 cm), male more colorful and longer-finned.

Tank/Water: $24 \times 12 \times 12$ in ($60 \times 30 \times 30$ cm), water types 2–6, 76–83°F (24–28°C).

Care: Keep in pairs in densely planted tanks furnished with floating plants. Males, especially cultivated forms, very aggressive toward each other. Keeping males singly in glasses—as was once the custom—is animal cruelty!

Habits: Surface fish found in weed-filled waters in Thailand, where it probably eats chiefly insect larvae.

Compatibility: With small barbs and bottom fish.

Similar species: Cultivated forms available from dealers.

12.5 gal

Siamese Tigerperch *Coius microlepis*
Also: *Datnioides microlepis*
Family: Coiidae, Datnioididae (see page 13).
Characteristics: 18 in (45 cm), hard to sex.
Tank/Water: 128 × 28 × 28 in (320 × 70 × 70 cm), water types 4–6, 76–83°F (24–28°C).

375 gal

Care: Peaceful fish, content in tanks furnished with lots of roots. Desirable to keep as a group. Feed highly nutritious live and frozen foods (shrimp, insects, fish).
Habits: Predator found in Southeast Asia in rivers, lakes, and flooded forests with many submerged branches. Protected species in Thailand!
Compatibility: Only with other giant fish, such as arowanas (*Scleropages*) and knifefish (*Chitala*).

Silver Arowana *Osteoglossum bicirrhosum*
Also: Silver arowana, arawana, aruana
Family: Bonytongues, Osteoglossidae (see page 7).
Characteristics: 48 in (120 cm), male has longer lower jaw.
Tank/Water: 80 × 60 × 28 in (450 × 150 × 70 cm), water types 2–5, 79–85°F (26–29°C).

1125 gal

Care: Adults are suitable only for display aquariums. Plantings along sides, some roots, but mainly ample swimming space for this fish, which constantly moves in circles. Takes fish meat and insects.
Habits: Lives near surface and hunts large insects and fish in large rivers and lakes of the Amazon basin.
Compatibility: With large, peaceful fish of Amazonia: rays, large cichlids, giant catfish.

Silver Dollar *Metynnis hypsauchen*
Also: Tetra silver dollar, *Metynnis schreitmuelleri*
Family: Characins, Characidae (see page 16).
Characteristics: 6 in (15 cm), male somewhat plumper.
Tank/Water: 60 × 20 × 20 in (150 × 50 × 50 cm), water types 2–5, 76–83°F (24–28°C).

100 gal

Care: Striking characin for large, unplanted tanks offering open swimming space on the one hand, and shelter in the form of roots on the other hand. Feed green foods and plant-based dry foods.
Habits: Schooling fish (keep at least six specimens) found in large South American rivers and lakes. This herbivore eats grass.
Compatibility: In large tanks with peaceful large cichlids (such as *Geophagus*) and catfish (such as *Sorubim*).

Silver-Tip Tetra *Hasemania nana*
Also: *Hemigrammus nanus*
Family: Tetras, Characidae (see page 16).
Characteristics: 2 in (5 cm), female paler and plumper.
Tank/Water: 24 × 12 × 12 in (60 × 30 × 30 cm), water types 2–6, 74–81°F (23–27°C).
Care: Keep at least six to eight specimens in dark, loosely planted aquariums, but provide adequate swimming space in the foreground. Takes all smaller foods.
Habits: Schooling fish found in blackwater streams of eastern Brazil outside of Amazonia.
Compatibility: With dwarf cichlids, small suckermouth and callichthyid armored catfish, as well as small characins that prefer the upper tank regions (such as *Copella arnoldi*).

12.5 gal

Six-barred Panchax *Epiplatys sexfasciatus*
Also: *Epiplatys infrafasciatus*
Family: Killifish, Aplocheilidae (see page 19).
Characteristics: 4 in (10 cm), male larger and more colorful.
Tank/Water: 32 × 14 × 16 in (80 × 35 × 40 cm), water types 2–4, 74–83°F (23–28°C).
Care: One male with several females in tanks that are not too bright, furnished with floating plants or roots near the surface in parts. Feed insects, mosquito larvae, possibly also dry foods.
Habits: Insect-eating surface fish found in small streams in the lowland rain forest of Cameroon and Nigeria.
Compatibility: Robust companion fish for African dwarf cichlids, barbs, and characins.
Similar species: *Epiplatys fasciolatus,* 3.5 in (9 cm).

25 gal

Skunk Corydoras *Corydoras arcuatus*
Family: Callichthyid armored catfish (see page 9).
Characteristics: 2.4 in (6 cm), female plumper.
Tank/Water: 24 × 12 × 12 in (60 × 30 × 30 cm), water types 2–5, 74–83°F (23–28°C).
Care: Keep as a group in tanks with sand substrate in parts, loose plantings, and structures where the fish can go to rest. Feed fine live, frozen, and dry foods. Use special *Corydoras* food.
Habits: Gregarious fish from soft-bottomed waters in the drainage of the upper Amazon in Peru.
Compatibility: Ideal companion fish for South American fish of the middle and upper tank regions. In small tanks, not with cichlids.
Similar species: *C. metae* and *C. melini,* both about 2 in (5 cm).

12.5 gal

Skunk Loach *Botia morleti*

Family: Loaches, Cobitidae (see page 17).

Characteristics: 2.75 in (7 cm), hard to sex. Be careful when fishing it out—it has a small spine under each eye!

Tank/Water: 32 × 14 × 16 in (80 × 35 × 40 cm), water types 2–5, 77–86°F (25–30°C).

Care: Best kept in largish groups of about five or six specimens in aquariums with shelters made of stone slabs and roots. Feed live, frozen, and sometimes dry foods; if possible, small snails as well.

Habits: Common fish in mid-sized and larger rivers of Thailand and Malaysia. Consumes snails and insect larvae. Digs shelters.

Compatibility: Good companion for medium-sized fish, such as barbs and labyrinthfish.

25 gal

Slender Cichlid *Cyprichromis leptosoma*

Family: Cichlids, Cichlidae (see page 10).

Characteristics: 5 in (12 cm), male larger and colorful.

Tank/Water: 48 × 20 × 20 in (120 × 50 × 50 cm), water types 5–6, 77–81°F (25–27°C).

Care: No furnishings needed, apart from a sand substrate. Keep one or many males with several females. Feed foods containing small crustaceans (*Artemia, Cyclops*, etc.).

Habits: Open-water fish that eats plankton exclusively, for example, small crustaceans such as *Cyclops*. Maternal mouthbrooder; does not form pairs.

Compatibility: Sand cichlids, such as *Enantiopus*.

Similar species: *Cyprichromis pavo*, 5 in (12 cm).

75 gal

Slender Hemiodus *Hemiodopsis gracilis*

Also: *Hemiodus gracilis*

Family: Hemiodidae (see page 16).

Characteristics: 7 in (18 cm), female slightly plumper.

Tank/Water: 80 × 24 × 24 in (200 × 60 × 60 cm), water types 2–4, 76–83°F (24–28°C).

Care: In a school of about eight specimens in large, loosely planted tanks with lots of space to swim. Large-leaved plants provide protection. Varied diet of assorted frozen foods, also dry food.

Habits: Timid schooling fish widely distributed in larger streams and rivers of Amazonia.

Compatibility: With peaceful large cichlids or dwarf cichlids, other medium-sized characins, and catfish.

175 gal

Slender Humphead *Steatocranus tinanti*
Also: *Leptotilapia tinanti*
Family: Cichlids, Cichlidae (see page 10).
Characteristics: 5 in (12 cm), males grow larger, develop a bigger hump on the head, and have a wider mouth.
Tank/Water: 40 × 16 × 16 in (100 × 40 × 40 cm), water types 3–6, 76–83°F (24–28°C).

37.5 gal

Care: Keep in pairs in tanks with good water movement, and with open space on the bottom and some flat stones under which the fish can dig out brooding cavities. Feed chiefly small crustaceans and dry foods.
Habits: Usually found in open areas of the Lower Congo rapids. Pair-forming cavity brooder.
Compatibility: Good with a pair of Congo dwarf cichlids.

Smallscale Archer *Toxotes microlepis*
Family: Archerfish, Toxotidae (see page 12).
Characteristics: 7 in (18 cm), hard to sex. Differs from other *Toxotes* species in its smaller scales and a yellowish body color in parts.
Tank/Water: 80 × 28 × 28 in (200 × 70 × 70 cm), water types 5–7, 79–85°F (26–29°C).

250 gal

Care: As a group in large tanks with roots, lowered water level, and sufficient swimming space. Feed highly nutritious frozen foods and large insects.
Habits: Not a brackish-water fish like other archerfish species, but an inhabitant of Southeast Asian rivers. Shoots down insects from branches by "spitting."
Compatibility: With robust Asian fish.

South American Bumblebee Catfish *Microglanis iheringi*
Family: Antenna catfish, Pimelodidae (see page 9).
Characteristics: 2.75 in (7 cm), no known sex differences.
Tank/Water: 24 × 12 × 12 in (60 × 30 × 30 cm), water types 2–5, 76–83°F (24–28°C).

12.5 gal

Care: Tanks furnished with rocks and roots to provide lots of hiding places. Water movement should approximate conditions in the wild. Keep one or several specimens. Feed frozen or live red mosquito larvae, tubifex.
Habits: Found in Venezuelan streams with fast-flowing water that rushes over rocks and gravel. Eats insects, mainly ants. Lives hidden, seen in daytime only when feeding.
Compatibility: Easy to keep with all fish longer than 1.6 in (4 cm) that have the same water requirements.

197

South American Leaf Fish *Monocirrhus polyacanthus*

Family: Nandids, Nandidae (see page 13).
Characteristics: 3 in (8 cm), female somewhat plumper with spawn.
Tank/Water: 24 × 12 × 12 in (60 × 30 × 30 cm), water types 1–3, 79–85°F (26–29°C).
Care: Keep in pairs in small, dark tanks, if hiding places (roots, plantings of large-leaved plants, floating plants) are available. Accepts only small, live food fish or mosquito larvae.
Habits: Lives in the bank vegetation of mostly quiet waters in Amazonia. When lying in ambush for fish, it mimics submerged fallen leaves.
Compatibility: Best kept in a species tank.
Similar species: *Polycentrus schomburgkii,* 4 in (10 cm).

12.5 gal

Spike-tailed Paradise Fish *Pseudosphromenus cupanus*

Also: Black spike-tailed paradise fish
Family: Labyrinthfish, family Osphronemidae (see page 16).
Characteristics: 2.75 in (7 cm), male longer-finned.
Tank/Water: 24 × 12 × 12 in (60 × 30 × 30 cm), water types 2–6, 74–81°F (23–27°C).
Care: Easily satisfied species that displays its behavioral repertoire in dark, well-planted tanks. Keep in pairs, with each fish needing its own cave.
Habits: Very peaceful inhabitant of shallow, swampy waters in Southeast Asia (India, for example), where it hunts for insect larvae amid leaf litter and aquatic plants.
Compatibility: With calmer rasboras and danios of the upper tank region, such as *Rasbora dorsiocellata.*

12.5 gal

Splash Tetra *Copella arnoldi*

Family: Lebiasinidae (see page 16).
Characteristics: 2.75 in (7 cm), male larger, longer-finned.
Tank/Water: 24 × 12 × 12 in (60 × 30 × 30 cm), water types 2–5, 76–85°F (24–29°C).
Care: Keep a few males with several females in tanks whose water surface is lowered to about 4 in (10 cm) under the cover pane. Floating plants. Let terrestrial plants (pothos) grow across the surface.
Habits: Surface fish found near the banks of clear streams in the Guyanas (South America). The males spawn with the females above the water, on the leaves of terrestrial plants, and spray the eggs with water from below.
Compatibility: Companion fish for dwarf cichlids.

12.5 gal

Spot-finned Spiny Eel *Macrognathus siamensis*

Also: Peacock eel, *Macrognathus aculeatus*
Family: Spiny eels, Mastacembelidae (see page 21).
Characteristics: 12 in (30 cm), female has plumper abdomen.
Tank/Water: 48 × 20 × 20 in (120 × 50 × 50 cm), water types 2–5, 74–81°F (23–27°C).

75 gal

Care: Planted tanks with floating-plant cover and hiding places. Fine gravel or sandy substrate suitable for burrowing. Feed mosquito larvae, fish meat, *Artemia*. Keep singly or in groups.
Habits: Inquisitive fish that inhabits slow-flowing or standing waters with soft bottoms in Southeast Asia. Nocturnal predators.
Compatibility: With all good-sized Asian fish species that live in the upper tank regions.

Spotted Blue-Eye *Pseudomugil gertrudae*

Family: Blue-eyes, Pseudomugilidae (see page 18).
Characteristics: 1.5 in (4 cm), female colorless, has shorter fins.
Tank/Water: 24 × 12 × 12 in (60 × 30 × 30 cm), water types 2–5, 77–83°F (25–28°C).

12.5 gal

Care: Group fish (two to three males with six or more females) for densely planted tanks with low water movement and with dim lighting. Feed small live or frozen foods (fruit flies, *Artemia*, *Cyclops*).
Habits: Inhabits shady rain forest streams, swamps, water-lily ponds in the rain forests of Australia and New Guinea.
Compatibility: Keep only with other dainty fish, such as *Trichopsis pumila*. Also with small fish of the bottom zone, such as small callichthyid armored catfish.

Spotted Climbing Perch *Ctenopoma acutirostre*

Family: Climbing perches, Anabantidae (see page 16).
Characteristics: 6 in (15 cm), male has spines behind the eyes.
Tank/Water: 48 × 20 × 20 in (120 × 50 × 50 cm), water types 2–5, 77–83°F (25–28°C).

75 gal

Care: Keep as a group in spacious tanks with root tangles and planted in parts with large-leaved plants. Feed live and dead fish, large insects, and cichlid sticks as well.
Habits: Lurking predators that hide under wood and wait for prey in rivers and lakes of the Congo basin. They can extend their mouths to suddenly suck in the prey.
Compatibility: Keep only with larger species, such as Congo tetras or larger naked catfish.
Similar species: *Ctenopoma kingsleyae,* 10 in (25 cm).

Spotted Headstander *Chilodus punctatus*
Family: Headstanders, Anostomidae (see page 16).
Characteristics: 3.5 in (9 cm), male slimmer.
Tank/Water: $40 \times 16 \times 16$ in ($100 \times 40 \times 40$ cm), water types 2–4, 76–83°F (24–28°C).
Care: Keep as a group of six to eight specimens in tanks with lots of structures (roots, slate slabs, large-leaved plants such as *Anubias,* Java fern). This plant eater requires green foods (blanched lettuce leaves, spinach), and frozen animal foods as well.
Habits: Found head down among plants and roots in various waters of the upper Amazon system.
Compatibility: With robust and/or agile South American species: suckermouth and callichthyid armored catfish, moderately sized cichlids. No angelfish.

37.5 gal

Spotted Hillstream Loach *Gastromyzon sp.*
Also: *Gastromyzon punctulatus, Gastromyzon borneensis*
Family: River loaches, family Balitoridae (see page 17).
Characteristics: 2.4 in (6 cm), male may have more colorful dorsal fin.
Tank/Water: $24 \times 12 \times 12$ in ($60 \times 30 \times 30$ cm), water types 2–5, 72–77°F (22–25°C).
Care: Keep several specimens in strongly lit tanks furnished with pebbles. Despite their prominent suckermouth, these loaches are not algae eaters; they need food tables and fine frozen foods (*Cyclops*).
Habits: Cool hill streams of Borneo. Not algae eaters. Each one defends its small "habitual place."
Compatibility: Small rasboras and danios.

12.5 gal

Spotted Raphael Catfish *Agamyxis albomaculatus*
Also: *Agamyxis pectinifrons*
Family: Thorny catfish, Doradidae (see page 9).
Characteristics: 6.3 in (16 cm), no sexual differences known.
Tank/Water: $32 \times 14 \times 16$ in ($80 \times 35 \times 40$ cm), water types 2–5, 77–85°F (25–29°C).
Care: Keep one or several in dark tanks with sandy substrate in parts and with hiding places. After turning off lighting, feed highly nutritious frozen foods or food tablets. Do not overfeed.
Habits: Nocturnal species from Amazonia.
Compatibility: With all fish that are not too small and have similar water requirements.
Similar species: Striped Raphael, *Platydoras costatus*, 8.6 in (22 cm).

25 gal

Starlight Bushynose Catfish *Ancistrus dolichopterus*

Also: Starlight pleco, *Ancistrus cf. hoplogenys*
Family: Suckermouth armored catfish, Loricariidae (see page 9).
Characteristics: 6 in (15 cm), male has snout tentacles.
Tank/Water: 40 × 16 × 16 in (100 × 40 × 40 cm), water types 1–2, 81–85°F (27–29°C).
Care: In pairs in tanks with subdued lighting, many wood roots to rasp on, and caves as hiding places, for example, the terra-cotta catfish caves sold in pet stores. Unlike the "normal" *Ancistrus sp.*, this species requires soft-water conditions. Feed plant foods, small crustaceans, and food tablets.
Habits: In submerged tangles of dead wood in the Rio Negro.
Compatibility: *Ancistrus* for blackwater tanks, for example, with angelfish, dwarf cichlids, and characins.

37.5 gal

Sterba's Cory *Corydoras sterbai*

Family: Callichthyid armored catfish, Callichthyidae (see page 9).
Characteristics: 2.4 in (6 cm), female plumper.
Tank/Water: 32 × 14 × 16 in (80 × 35 × 40 cm), water types 2–5, 74–79°F (23–26°C).
Care: Keep as a group in tanks with sandy substrate in parts, loose plantings, and structures where the fish can go to rest. Like many other armored catfish, they enjoy gentle water movement. Feed fine live, frozen, and dry foods. Use special food for *Corydoras*!
Habits: Very gregarious fish native to soft-bottomed areas of the waters of the Rio Guaporé in Brazil.
Compatibility: Companion for South American fish of the middle and upper tank regions. Not with cichlids.

25 gal

Striped Goby Cichlid *Eretmodus cyanostictus*

Family: Cichlids, Cichlidae (see page 10).
Characteristics: 4 in (10 cm), hard to sex.
Tank/Water: 40 × 16 × 16 in (100 × 40 × 40 cm), water types 5–6, 77–81°F (25–27°C).
Care: Keep in pairs in strongly lit tanks furnished with rocks and pebbles. Feed exclusively fiber-rich foods (shrimp mixes and dry food containing *Spirulina*). Water movement beneficial.
Habits: Pair-forming mouthbrooder; lives in rock debris in the surge habitat of Lake Tanganyika. Algae eater.
Compatibility: Good with *Tropheus* species. Not with species that need other foods as a high-fiber diet, because *Eretmodus* does not tolerate other foods.
Similar species: *Tanganicodus irascae*, 2.75 in (7 cm).

37.5 gal

Striped Headstander *Anostomus anostomus*

Family: Headstanders, Anostomidae (see page 16).
Characteristics: 7 in (18 cm), females grow bigger and plumper.
Tank/Water: 64 × 24 × 24 in (160 × 60 × 60 cm), water types 2–4, 76–83°F (24–28°C).
Care: Keep singly or in a large group of 10–12 specimens. Each one needs a shelter (roots, for example). Feed plant foods, fine frozen foods; dry food alone is insufficient.
Habits: Group fish found in larger flowing water bodies with rocks or dead wood in northern South America.
Compatibility: Can annoy slow fish, such as angelfish. Otherwise, only with peaceful fish, such as large suckermouth armored catfish or characins.

150 gal

Striped Loach *Botia striata*

Also: Zebra loach, candy-stripe loach, thin-line loach
Family: Loaches, Cobitidae (see page 17).
Characteristics: 3 in (8 cm), hard to sex. Be careful when you catch this fish—there's a small spine under each eye!
Tank/Water: 32 × 14 × 16 in (80 × 35 × 40 cm), water types 2–5, 74–81°F (23–27°C).
Care: Keep several specimens in loosely planted tanks with a few shelters. Sandy substrate in parts allows this fish to burrow. Eats small snails and can be used in an aquarium to control snails.
Habits: Peaceful snail eater, indigenous to India.
Compatibility: Ideal bottom fish for Asian community tanks with barbs, rasboras and danios, and labyrinthfish that inhabit the upper tank regions.

25 gal

Striped Panchax *Aplocheilus lineatus*

Family: Killifish, family Aplocheilidae (see page 19).
Characteristics: 5 in (12 cm), male larger and more colorful.
Tank/Water: 32 × 14 × 16 in (80 × 35 × 40 cm), water types 2–6, 76–85°F (24–29°C).
Care: One male with several females in tanks that are densely planted in parts (floating plants). Important: Feed insects (small house crickets, flies, etc.).
Habits: Predatory surface fish found in many different water types in India, where it lies in wait for insects and young fish. Males aggressive toward each other.
Compatibility: Only with somewhat larger, peaceful fish of other tank regions, such as Asian barbs (*Puntius*) or loaches (such as *Botia*).

25 gal

Striped Peckoltia *Peckoltia cf. vittata*

Family: Suckermouth armored catfish, Loricariidae (see page 9).
Characteristics: 3 in (8 cm), male has "gill spines."
Tank/Water: 24 × 12 × 12 in (60 × 30 × 30 cm), water types
2–5, 77–85°F (25–29°C).

12.5 gal

Care: Keep in pairs in dark tanks with many roots and narrow
caves made of roots or clay tubes barely large enough to
accommodate the fish. Feed green and dry foods, as well as
frozen small crustaceans.
Habits: Found in tangles of dead wood in the Rio Negro
(Brazil, Venezuela); males defend caves during spawning period.
Compatibility: Other suckermouth armored catfish and all
smaller fish with similar water requirements.

Sutchi Catfish *Pangasius hypophthalmus*

Also: Iridescent shark, *Pangasius sutchi*
Family: Giant catfish, Pangasidae (see page 9).
Characteristics: 52 in (130 cm), pretty color present only in
juveniles.
Tank/Water: Circular tank with at least 1,500-gal (6,000-L)
capacity; using smaller tanks is animal cruelty. Water types
3–5, 74–83°F (23–28°C).

1500 gal

Care: Peaceful group fish that loves to swim, can be appropri-
ately kept only in huge tanks. Feed pellets.
Habits: Inhabits large rivers in Asia, such as the Mekong. Eats
mainly other fish, crustaceans, and half-decayed organic mater
(detritus). The species migrates to spawning and feeding sites.
Compatibility: With large fish, such as *Barbodes*.

Swordtail *Xiphophorus helleri*

Family: Live-bearing toothcarp of the Poeciliidae (see page 20).
Characteristics: 5 in (12 cm), male has "sword" and copulatory organ.
Tank/Water: 40 × 16 × 16 in (100 × 40 × 40 cm), water types
4–6, 72–83°F (22–28°C).

37.5 gal

Care: Group fish (one male with several females, or a great
many males); two males will fight too much. Brightly lit aquariums with water movement.
Habits: Wild forms found in flowing waters of Mexico and
Guatemala, where they graze on algae growing on rocks.
Compatibility: As in the wild, with smaller Central American
cichlids (such as small *Thorichthys* or *Archocentius* species), but
also with catfish, characins, etc.

Swordtail Characin *Corynopoma riisei*
Family: Characins, Characidae (see page 16).
Characteristics: 2.75 in (7 cm), males have enlarged fins and spoon-like gill-cover extensions.
Tank/Water: 24 × 12 × 12 in (60 × 30 × 30 cm), water types 2–5, 76–85°F (24–29°C).
Care: Lively schooling fish that needs lots of open swimming space, loose plantings along the tank sides, and good water movement. Takes all standard food types.
Habits: Smooth-running coastal rivers and streams in northern South America and Trinidad. Males have interesting courtship behavior in which they wave their elongated gill-cover structures jerkily in view of the females.
Compatibility: With smaller fish of the lower tank regions.

12.5 gal

Thick-lipped Gourami *Colisa labiosa*
Family: Gouramis, family Osphronemidae (see page 16).
Characteristics: 3.5 in (9 cm), male more colorful.
Tank/Water: 32 × 14 × 16 in (80 × 35 × 40 cm), water types 2–6, 72–83°F (22–28°C).
Care: Keep in pairs in loosely planted aquariums with a few roots that extend to the water surface and a cover of floating plants. Feed high-nutrient flaked food and occasionally live food. No water movement.
Habits: Native to quiet areas of rivers and swamps in southern Myanmar (Burma). Probably eats insect larvae and small animals.
Compatibility: With relatively calm fish of the lower tank strata, such as river loaches and small barbs.
Similar species: Giant gourami, *C. fasciata*, 5 in (12 cm).

25 gal

Threadfin Acara *Acarichthys heckelli*
Family: Cichlids, Cichlidae (see page 10).
Characteristics: 10 in (25 cm), female smaller, shorter-finned.
Tank/Water: 80 × 24 × 24 in (200 × 60 × 60 cm), water types 2–4, 77–83°F (25–28°C).
Care: Tanks decorated with roots and rocks and equipped with about 6-in (15-cm) wide and 12-in (30-cm) long tubes to accommodate their natural habits. Feed highly nutritious live, frozen, and dry foods. It is best to keep a group of six to eight specimens.
Habits: In various water types in Amazonia, digs tunnels that serve as spawning sites for the eggs. Pair-forming cavity brooder.
Compatibility: With large characins and suckermouth armored catfish, as well as peaceful cichlids, such as *Heros*.

175 gal

Threadfin Rainbow *Iriatherina werneri*
Family: Rainbowfish, Melanotaeniidae (see page 18).
Characteristics: 2 in (5 cm), male has very elongated fins and much more intense colors.
Tank/Water: 32 × 14 × 16 in (80 × 35 × 40 cm), water types 2–5, 77–86°F (25–30°C).
Care: Group fish for densely planted tanks. Feed fine live foods (*Artemia* nauplii, *Cyclops,* and water fleas) and dry foods.
Habits: Found in plant-rich ponds and still stretches of flowing waters in southern New Guinea and northern Australia.
Compatibility: Good companion fish for small bottom-dwelling fish, such as callichthyid armored catfish. Do not keep with other larger fish.

25 gal

Three-lined Cory *Corydoras trilineatus*
Also: *Corydoras julii*
Family: Callichthyid armored catfish, Callichthyidae (see page 9).
Characteristics: 2.4 in (6 cm), female plumper.
Tank/Water: 24 × 12 × 12 in (60 × 30 × 30 cm), water types 2–5, 77–83°F (25–28°C).
Care: Keep as a group in tanks with sand substrate in parts, loose plantings, and structures that offer a resting place. Feed fine live, frozen, and dry foods. Use special *Corydoras* food!
Habits: Gregarious fish from soft-bottomed stretches of waters in the Peruvian Amazon region.
Compatibility: Ideal companion for South American fish of the middle and upper tank regions. In small tanks, not with cichlids.

12.5 gal

Three-striped African Glass Catfish *Pareutropius buffei*
Also: *Eutropiellus buffei*
Family: Glass catfish, Schilbeidae (see page 9).
Characteristics: 3 in (8 cm), female plumper.
Tank/Water: 40 × 16 × 16 in (100 × 40 × 40 cm), water types 2–5, 76–83°F (24–28°C).
Care: In bright tanks with strong water movement, loose plantings, and root shelters. Feed all smaller foods. Keep at least six specimens.
Habits: Lively schooling fish found in fast-flowing stretches along the banks of largish clearwater rivers in Nigeria.
Compatibility: Ideal companion fish for the open-water area of an African tank, for example, with small naked catfish (*Synodontis*) and cichlids (*Pelvicachromis*).

37.5 gal

Tiger Barb *Puntius tetrazona*
Also: Sumatra barb
Family: Carp and minnows, Cyprinidae (see page 16).
Characteristics: 2.75 in (7 cm), male has more intense coloring.
Tank/Water: $40 \times 20 \times 20$ in ($100 \times 50 \times 50$ cm), water types 2–6, 74–83°F (23–28°C).

62.5 gal

Care: Keep at least 8–12 specimens and always provide ample food. If you keep too few, they often bother other fish, probably out of "boredom." Feed all standard food types; don't forget green foods, such as lettuce leaves, for nibbling.
Habits: Extremely lively and restless-seeming group fish found in the bottom area of slow-flowing and standing waters in Sumatra (Indonesia).
Compatibility: Only with hardy and also lively species.

Tinfoil Barb *Barbodes schwanenfeldii*
Also: *Puntius schwanenfeldi, Barbus schwanenfeldi*
Family: Carp and minnows, Cyprinidae (see page 16).
Characteristics: 14 in (35 cm), female plumper.
Tank/Water: $128 \times 24 \times 24$ in ($320 \times 60 \times 60$ cm), water types 2–5, 72–83°F (22–28°C).

300 gal

Care: In large aquariums with lots of room to swim, sand substrate, and a few roots. Feed plant-based dry food, all standard food types.
Habits: Robust species found in a wide variety of water types in Southeast Asia. In the wild, mainly herbivorous. Popular as a food fish.
Compatibility: Only with other larger fish species. Small fish are occasionally eaten.

Triangle Cichlid *Uaru amphiacanthoides*
Family: Cichlids, Cichlidae (see page 10).
Characteristics: 10 in (25 cm), hard to sex.
Tank/Water: $80 \times 24 \times 24$ in ($200 \times 60 \times 60$ cm), water types 1–3, 79–86°F (26–30°C).

175 gal

Care: As a group (at least six specimens) in large, dark tanks with lots of dead wood, which the fish nibble at. Plenty of green foods (zucchini, lettuce) and plant-based dry foods. Heavy filtration.
Habits: Herbivorous cichlid found in Amazonia, in larger water bodies containing plenty of wood. Pair-forming open spawner.
Compatibility: Excellent companion for peaceful large fish of South America.

Twig Catfish *Farlowella sp.*

Family: Suckermouth armored catfish, Loricariidae (see page 9).
Characteristics: 6–10 in (15–25 cm) (depending on species), male has facial "whiskers."
Tank/Water: 32 × 14 × 16 in (80 × 35 × 40 cm), water types 2–5, 77–83°F (25–28°C).

25 gal

Care: In pairs in tanks with lots of roots. Several males will compete for food, and the loser will perish. Feed daily: plant foods, food tablets, and frozen animal foods (such as *Cyclops*).
Habits: Found on twigs and small sticks lying near the banks of Amazonian streams and rivers. Their body shape provides excellent camouflage. They eat algae and small food animals.
Compatibility: Only with very small companions that do not compete with them for food, such as neons.

Upside-Down Catfish *Synodontis nigriventris*

Family: Naked catfish, Mochokidae (see page 9).
Characteristics: 3 in (8 cm), female plumper when ready to spawn.
Tank/Water: 40 × 16 × 16 in (100 × 40 × 40 cm), water types 2–5, 76–83°F (24–28°C).

37.5 gal

Care: Group fish for densely planted tanks furnished with roots and many shelters. Omnivore with preference for black mosquito larvae.
Habits: Gregarious fish found near plant-rich banks of larger rivers and swamps in the Congo rain forest. Eats insect larvae.
Compatibility: Ideal companion fish for Congo tanks with dwarf cichlids (*Nanochromis*) and characins (such as *Phenacogrammus, Bathyaethiops*).

Whiptail Catfish *Rineloricaria lanceolata*

Also: Lanceolate whiptail catfish, *Hemiloricaria lanceolata*
Family: Suckermouth armored catfish, Loricariidae (see page 9).
Characteristics: 5.25 in (13 cm), male has whiskers.
Tank/Water: 32 × 12 × 12 in (80 × 30 × 30 cm), water types 2–5, 76–83°F (24–28°C).

20 gal

Care: In pairs in tanks with clear water, sand, and some elongated roots. Feed plant foods, frozen small crustaceans, food tablets.
Habits: On and under branches lying in the current of small, clear flowing waters in the Amazon region.
Compatibility: With smaller characins and dwarf cichlids (such as *Apistogramma*) from South America.
Similar species: *Rineloricaria sp.* "Red," 5 in (12 cm).

White Cloud Mountain Minnow *Tanichthys albonubes*

Family: Carp and minnows, Cyprinidae (see page 16).
Characteristics: 1.5 in (4 cm), male more intensely colored.
Tank/Water: 24 × 12 × 12 in (60 × 30 × 30 cm), water types 2–6, 65–72°F (18–22°C).

12.5 gal

Care: Undemanding schooling fish (at least 8-10 specimens) for loosely planted tanks that are not too brightly lit. If kept too warm, this fish will lose its lovely colors and its vitality. Standard foods.
Habits: Stream-dwelling group fish native to hill streams, where it probably hunts insects and their larvae.
Compatibility: With bottom-dwelling stream fish from Asia, such as stream loaches or hillstream loaches.

White-spotted Tropheus *Tropheus duboisi*

Family: Cichlids, Cichlidae (see page 10).
Characteristics: 5.25 in (13 cm), hard to sex.
Tank/Water: 60 × 24 × 24 in (150 × 60 × 60 cm), water types 5–6, 77–81°F (25–27°C).

137.5 gal

Care: Keep a few males with many females in strongly lit tanks. Feed only high-fiber foods, such as food mixes containing *Spirulina*, algae, and shrimp. Red mosquito larvae and overly protein-rich diet will be fatal!
Habits: Found in shallow water in the rock area of Lake Tanganyika that gets heavy sun. Algae eater. Maternal mouthbrooder; does not form pairs.
Compatibility: With *Tropheus moorii.* Never with fish that require low-fiber foods.

Worm-jawed Mormyrid *Campylomormyrus tamandua*

Family: Elephant noses or mormyrids, Mormyridae (see page 7).
Characteristics: 17 in (43 cm), male has concave anal fin.
Tank/Water: 128 × 24 × 24 in (320 × 60 × 60 cm), water types 2–5, 77–85°F (25–29°C).

300 gal

Care: Keep two males and three females in tanks with lots of hiding places (one per fish). Feed highly nutritious foods in the evening or, preferably, at night, frozen red mosquito larvae.
Habits: Nocturnal species from rocky and turbulent stretches of the Niger and Congo rivers. Uses its pincerlike mouth to hunt for insect larvae in recesses in the rock. Communicates and finds its way with weak electrical charges. Aggressive with others of its species.
Compatibility: With peaceful tetras.

Wrestling Halfbeak *Dermogenys pusilla*
Also: *Dermogenys pusillus*, **Siamese halfbeak**
Family: Halfbeaks, Hemirhamphidae (see page 18).
Characteristics: 3 in (8 cm), male has colorful fins.
Tank/Water: $32 \times 14 \times 16$ in ($80 \times 35 \times 40$ cm), water types 5–6, 79–83°F (24–28°C).

25 gal

Care: Keep as a group (in smaller tanks, one male with several females) in tanks with gentle surface water movement and loose plantings along the sides. Must be fed insect foods (black mosquito larvae, *Drosophila*). Males prone to fight.
Habits: Insect-eating surface fish found in shallow waters near coasts of Southeast Asia. Also in brackish water.
Compatibility: With smaller Asian brackish-water fish, such as bumblebee gobies.

Xenotilapia papilio
Family: Cichlids, Cichlidae (see page 10).
Characteristics: 3.5 in (9 cm), hard to sex.
Tank/Water: $40 \times 20 \times 20$ in ($100 \times 50 \times 50$ cm), water types 5–6, 77–81°F (25–27°C).

62.5 gal

Care: Groups of at least six specimens, from which pairs can form. Set up tanks with swimming space over sandy areas and a few rocks. Feed dry foods, small crustaceans, and shrimp mixes.
Habits: Extracts food from the sediment over rocks in Lake Tanganyika. Pair-forming mouthbrooder.
Compatibility: Lake Tanganyikan cichlids, such as *Cyprichromis*, in tanks with rocks piled up in the background also *Julidochromis* and small *Neolamprologus*.
Similar species: *Xenotilapia spilopterus*, 4 in (10 cm).

X-Ray Tetra *Pristella maxillaries*
Also: Pristella tetra, *Pristella riddlei*
Family: Tetras, Characidae (see page 16).
Characteristics: 1.75 in (4.5 cm), female plumper.
Tank/Water: $24 \times 12 \times 12$ in ($60 \times 30 \times 30$ cm), water types 2–4, 76–81°F (24–27°C).

12.5 gal

Care: Undemanding schooling fish for densely planted aquariums with soft to moderately hard water. Feed all standard foods.
Habits: Widely distributed in South America, in swamp waters densely covered with water lilies, where it probably eats small crustaceans, mosquito larvae, and insects.
Compatibility: Good companion fish for callichthyid armored catfish and, in larger tanks, for dwarf cichlids.
Similar species: *Hyphessobrycon roseus*, 1.2 in (3 cm).

Yellow Congo Characin *Alestopetersius caudalis*
Also: *Phenacogrammus, Hemigrammopetersius caudalis*
Family: True African tetras, Alestiidae (see page 16).
Characteristics: 2.75 in (7 cm), male more colorful, with bigger fins.
Tank/Water: 40 × 16 × 16 in (100 × 40 × 40 cm), water types 2–5, 74–81°F (23–27°C).
Care: Keep about eight specimens in loosely planted tanks furnished with some roots. Dim lighting and dark substrate. Especially fond of black mosquito larvae and fruit flies, but also accepts other small frozen and dry foods.
Habits: Schooling fish, loves to swim, found in clear flowing waters of the Congo basin. Eats insects.
Compatibility: With catfish and dwarf cichlids.

37.5 gal

Yellow Labidochromis *Labidochromis sp. "yellow"*
Also: *Labidochromis caeruleus "yellow"*
Family: Cichlids, Cichlidae (see page 10).
Characteristics: 4 in (10 cm), hard to sex.
Tank/Water: 40 × 20 × 20 in (100 × 50 × 50 cm), water types 5–6, 77–81°F (25–27°C).
Care: One or many males with several females in a tank furnished with rocks. Arrange the rock clusters so that the fish can swim through all the openings. All foods, especially food containing small crustaceans.
Habits: At a depth of 50–66 ft (15–20 m) in a narrowly defined rocky part of Lake Malawi. Eats insect larvae. Maternal mouthbrooder; does not form pairs.
Compatibility: With other rock-dwelling cichlids.

62.5 gal

Yellow Marbled Syno *Synodontis schoutedeni*
Family: Naked catfish, Mochokidae (see page 9).
Characteristics: 6.7 in (17 cm), female is plumper.
Tank/Water: 48 × 20 × 20 in (120 × 50 × 50 cm), water types 2–5, 77–83°F (25–28°C).
Care: Tank furnished with lots of structures, including large-leaved plants and roots, and with fine-grained substrate. Feed frozen or live mosquito larvae and tablets or pellets. Keep singly or in a group of at least five specimens.
Habits: Lives in slow-flowing, often plant-rich streams and sections of rivers in the Congo basin. Unlike other naked catfish, also active during the day.
Compatibility: With fish of the Congo basin, such as Congo tetra species (*Phenacogrammus, Bathyaethiops*).

75 gal

Yellow-tailed Acei *Pseudotropheus sp. "acei"*

Family: Cichlids, Cichlidae (see page 10).
Characteristics: 5 in (12 cm), the yellow spots on the anal fin (egg spots) are more intensely colored in the males.
Tank/Water: 48 × 20 × 20 in (120 × 50 × 50 cm), water types 5–6, 77–81°F (25–27°C).

75 gal

Care: One or many males with several females in aquariums with root wood that has been well soaked in water and with *Vallisneria*. Takes high-fiber dry food, small crustaceans.
Habits: Inhabits sandy areas of Lake Malawi. Eats chiefly algae growing on wood surfaces, such as trees that have fallen into the water. Maternal mouthbrooder; does not form pairs.
Compatibility: With bristlenose catfish and cuckoo catfish, as well as *Copadichromis borleyi*.

Zebra Danio *Danio rerio*

Also: Zebrafish, *Brachydanio rerio*
Family: Carp and minnows, Cyprinidae (see page 16).
Characteristics: About 2.4 in (6 cm), male slimmer.
Tank/Water: 32 × 14 × 16 in (80 × 35 × 40 cm), water types 2–6, 74–81°F (23–27°C).

25 gal

Care: Keep in a school in elongated, light aquariums with strong water movement and gravelly substrate, with a few pebbles. Takes all standard foods.
Habits: Very lively stream fish from clear streams in northern India; loves to swim.
Compatibility: Ideal with bottom-dwelling stream fish from Asia, such as stream loaches (*Schistura, Nemacheilus*) or hill-stream loaches (*Gastromyzon*).

Zebra Pleco *Hypancistrus zebra*

Family: Suckermouth armored catfish, Loricariidae (see page 9).
Characteristics: 3.5 in (9 cm), large males have small spines (odontodes) on their cheeks and pectoral fins.
Tank/Water: 24 × 12 × 12 in (60 × 30 × 30 cm), water types 2–5, 81–86°F (27–30°C).

12.5 gal

Care: Sufficient warm water is the most important requirement, in addition to pebbles, stone slabs, and good water movement. Feed primarily frozen foods, such as small crustaceans. Not an algae eater. Clay pipes especially for suckermouth armored catfish, available in pet stores, provide hiding places.
Habits: Found in rocky biotopes of the clearwater Rio Xingu in the Amazon. This species lives in concealment.
Compatibility: With other clearwater fish.

Shrimp and Crabs and Crayfish

In the past few years, brilliantly colored and bizarre freshwater crustaceans have become huge hits in the aquarium hobby. Many species are ideal aquarium pets that can also be kept in community tanks with fish, provided you keep a few rules in mind:

➤ Provide a varied diet (see TIP at right).

➤ Furnish the tank with an ample number of hiding places (except for dwarf shrimp, at least one hiding place—such as a narrow bamboo tube—for each specimen).

➤ Never keep them in newly set-up tanks.

➤ Most species are more sensitive than fish in their reaction to chemical loads in the water, caused, for example, by copper water pipes or fish medications.

➤ Regular water changes and aquarium water that is high in oxygen and not organically loaded are very important, just as they are for fish.

➤ Because these creatures are so good at climbing, tight-fitting cover panes are essential. For larger species, the cover must be weighted down.

➤ Crustaceans have a hard shell, or exoskeleton, that does not grow along with them, so from time to time they shed or molt their outer covering. Leave the discarded covering in the tank for a while (see TIP below).

➤ Compatibility differs, depending on the species (see TIP, page 20).

Red mangrove crabs (2 in [5 cm]) need an opportunity to come out onto dry land.

TIP

Feeding Crustaceans
A varied diet of different types of live and frozen foods (mosquito larvae, *Cyclops, Artemia* nauplii), as well as dry and green foods. Mangrove crabs and prawns love cooked fish. Fan shrimp catch fine live and dry foods in the current, but will also accept other foods. Adding dry beech leaves regularly is important for the molting process!

1 Red swamp crayfish

2 Redclaw shrimp

3 Louisiana dwarf crayfish

Moluccan fan shrimp

5 Crystal Red dwarf shrimp

Cameroon armored shrimp

Bee shrimp 7

8 Fire shrimp

Some especially popular species are pictured on pages 228/229. In your care, these species require the conditions outlined below:

Red mangrove crabs: 24 × 12 × 12 in (60 × 30 × 30 cm) tank for a pair (female has larger abdominal flap). Water types 6–7—(see page 24), 72–77°F (22–25°C). Small bit of dry land, such as cork bark. At least 4 in (10 cm) of air space between water surface and cover pane—(see photo, page 226).

Fan shrimp: 24 × 12 × 12 in (60 × 30 × 30 cm) tank for a single specimen, water types 3–6—(see page 24), 74–79°F (23–26°C). These are current-loving species. Very peaceful—see page 229; Moluccan

> Amano shrimp (1.6 in [4 cm]) are fond of eating thread algae.

TIP

Compatibility
Although all crustaceans have claws that can exert great pressure, most of them make good tank-mates even for very small fish. The *Machobrachium* species are an exception, as they will attack smaller fish and other crustaceans, especially at night. If you want a species tank, you need enough hiding places for each specimen.

fan shrimp, *Atyopsis molluc-
censis,* 4 in (10 cm);
Cameroon armored shrimp,
Atya gabonensis, 6 in (15 cm).

Redclaw shrimp: 24 × 12 ×
12 in (60 × 30 × 30 cm) tank is
adequate for one male and two
or three females. Water types
3–6—(see page 24), 68–81°F
(20–27°C). Predatory species
that can pose a threat to its
tankmates—see page 228: redclaw shrimp, *Macrobrachium
assamensis,* 3 in (8 cm).

Dwarf shrimp (*Caridina* or
Neocaridina species): For
smaller species, a tank at least

12 × 8 × 8 in (30 × 20 × 20
cm) for a group of five specimens; for larger species, 16 ×
10 × 10 in (40 × 25 × 25 cm).
Water types 3–6—see page
24), 74–79°F (23–26°C)—see
photos on page 229: crystal
red shrimp, *Neocaridina sp.*
"Crystal Red," 1 in (2.5 cm);
fire shrimp, *Neocaridina sp.*
"Fire," 1 in (2.5 cm); bee
shrimp, *Neocaridina sp.*
"Biene," 1.2 in (3 cm).

River crayfish (*Procambarus*
and *Camberellus* species): five
specimens of the dwarf
species in 12 × 8 × 8 in (30 ×
20 × 20 cm) tanks; one or
two specimens of the larger
species in 26-gal (100-L)
tanks. Water types 3–6—see
page 24), 50–86°F (10–30°C).
Never keep in a garden pond:
danger of reintroduction to
the wild! See photos on page
228: red swamp crayfish, *Procambarus clarkii,* 5 in (12 cm);
dwarf crayfish, *Cambarellus
shufeldtii,* 1.2 in (3 cm).

**African dwarf frog,
Hymenochiris cf.
boettgeri (1.4 in [3.5 cm]).**

1 > Trumpet snail

2 > Murex snail

3 > Large pond snail

4 > Ramshorn snail

Apple snail 5 >

Snails in the Aquarium

Snails can greatly add to the variety in an aquarium. Several species have become true fixtures in the aquarium hobby, in some cases because they are especially pretty to look at. These include, for example, the apple snails (*Pomacea, Asolene,* and *Marisa* species) and certain trumpet snails with small, low spines.

However, snails can also perform useful functions in an aquarium. The burrowing trumpet snails (*Melanoides* species), for example, occupy the same niche in the aquarium substrate as do the earthworms in the garden—they aerate the substrate and recycle organic waste products, thus promoting good plant growth. Other species, such as the ramshorn snails (*Planorbis* and *Planorbarius* and *Planorbella*), the large pond snails (*Lymnaea* species), or the various apple snail species, graze unceasingly on the substrate, searching for leftover food, and in this way they help prevent areas from decaying. That benefits the water quality.

In some cases, however, snails can also create a nuisance, when their numbers become too large—usually because the fish have been overfed. Then they can be reduced in number or removed (see TIP below).

Snails reproduce either by bearing fully formed young (live-bearing) or by laying gelatinous masses of eggs on plants or on the aquarium cover. If you put snails in your aquarium, make sure that you know how they reproduce, so that you don't accidently destroy any eggs.

TIP

Snail Plague
Sometimes snails undergo an explosive increase in number. They are not harmful, except in breeding tanks or in tanks with very delicate aquatic plants. To combat the plague, use only natural means—pet stores sell special traps, or you can put snail-eating fish, such as clown loaches, in your aquarium, if they are a suitable match for the other inhabitants.

Biotope
Aquariums

So-called biotope aquariums are
set up with the idea of duplicating
the flora and fauna of a natural
habitat. Here you will find, as
examples, five suggested tank
setups that will make you want an
aquarium that is just like nature.

South American Tank

Biotope: The tank should portray a quiet section of water in a clear, fairly large rain forest creek.

Population: A group of larger tetras, dwarf cichlids for the bottom stratum, a small group of angelfish, and a group of dwarf suckermouths (*Otocinclus affinis*) as algae eaters.

Tank: 48 × 20 × 20 in (120 × 50 × 50 cm).

Water: Water type 3 (see page 24).

Temperature: 79°F (26°C).

Lighting: Two daylight fluorescent lamps and one Grolux

> Bleeding heart tetra (*Hyphessobrycon erythrostigma*).

TIP

Leaves in the Aquarium

Many fish live along tree-covered banks. The leaves that fall into the water serve not only as food for insect larvae and crabs and crayfish, but also as places in which to hide and to spawn. Dried red beech leaves, soaked in water for a few days before being introduced, have proved their worth in aquariums.

(plant-growth) fluorescent lamp.

Water movement: Slight water movement through the filter intake of a power filter.

Decor/Plantings: In the foreground, cover one-fourth of the well-fertilized substrate of fine gravel with a layer of dried beech, oak, or rubber-tree leaves. Using relatively thin-branched roots (such as bog-pine roots that have been soaked in water), structure almost the entire rear third of the tank so that most of the root branches run vertically from top to bottom. The

Emperor tetras are an alternative to the bleeding heart tetras.

angelfish can use them as a place to retreat. In the middle tank stratum, position two large Amazon sword plants some distance apart.

Feeding: Once a day, frozen or live black, white, or red mosquito larvae, *Cyclops;* once a day, highly nutritious dry food; occasionally a weighted zucchini slice for the dwarf suckermouths. Be sure not to overfeed the fish by putting too much food in the tank.

Apistogramma dwarf cichlids enliven the bottom level.

Lake Malawi Rock Tank

Biotope: The tank should portray a clear, rocky section of the shore region of Lake Malawi.

Population: One male and three females of each of three species of different-colored rock cichlids (Mbuna), such as *Metriaclima, Pseudotropheus, Melanochromis, Labidochromis*. Not entirely appropriate to the biotope: algae-eating sucker-mouth armored catfish (bushynose catfish).

Tank: 48 × 20 × 20 in (120 × 50 × 50 cm).

Water: Water type 5 (see page 24).

Temperature: 79°F (26°C).

- ✔ for example, 1 male and 3 females of each of these species: red zebra, electric blue johanni, *Labidochromis sp. "yellow"*
- ✔ 1 pair of bristlenose catfish
- ✔ 30 twisted vallisnerias (if desired)
- ✔ Styrofoam slab .4 in (1 cm) thick to place under the bottom pane
- ✔ 50 to 100 rocks, such as honeycomb limestone

Rock zone of Lake Malawi with red zebras (*Metriaclima estherae*).

Mbuna Rock Cichlids
In their native habitat, the rock cichlids of Lake Malawi (Mbuna) eat the algae that thrive on rocks in the sunny shallow water, as well as the crustaceans and krill that live in it. The fish display their brilliant colors only when they have a balanced diet, which must be high in fiber and so-called carotinoids. A suitable food for rock cichlids is shrimp mix, available in frozen form in pet stores.

Electric blue johanni male. The female is orange in color.

Lighting: 2 to 3 daylight fluorescent lamps and one Grolux (plant-growth) fluorescent lamp.
Water movement: Moderate water movement through the power-filter outflow simulates the natural waves.
Décor/Plantings: On a .4-in (1-cm) thick Styrofoam slab in the background, pile up rock layers such as honeycomb limestone, so that they remain stable and almost reach the water surface. Construct the piles so as to create numerous passages for the fish to swim through. If you like, you can plant a few vallisnerias (not entirely biotope-appropriate). For the bushynose catfish, include a

Labidochromis sp. **"yellow" is a popular Lake Malawi cichlid.**

wood root to gnaw on.
Feeding: Feed adult Mbuna only every other day, with shrimp mix, *Cyclops, Mysis* shrimp, and *Spirulina* flakes.

Tank for Large Fish

> Oscars can reach a length of more than 16 in (40 cm).

Biotope: The tank should simulate a rocky section, containing driftwood, along the bank of an Amazon clearwater river.

Population: One group of oscars, one pair of large pike cichlids, three plecos (*Pseudacanthicus*), and one group of high-backed large characins.

Tank: 128 × 32 × 28 in (320 × 80 × 70 cm).

Water: Water type 2 (see page 24).

Temperature: 83°F (28°C).

Lighting: Four 70-watt HQI aquarium lights.

Water movement: Strong

TIP

All-Glass Aquariums
Today it is technically possible to seal all-glass aquariums with a capacity of several thousand liters. Once the load-bearing ability of the floor has been tested, these aquariums can even be set up in apartments. Such an aquarium, together with the equipment and furnishings, can easily weigh 3 tons! Pond-filter systems are the best type of filtration for such aquariums.

movement in parts, through centrifugal (rotary) pumps in the tank foreground.

Décor/Plantings: All the cichlids in this suggested population can plainly attain a length of more than 12 in (30 cm); therefore they need stable furnishings that their burrowing can't destroy. Provide a thick layer of fine gravel as the substrate, and in the tank background place large, elongated roots, piled up lengthwise on the substrate. The pike cichlids and scarlet cats need stable shelters in the form of large stone slabs. No plants.

Female orange pike cichlid. Once a pair is formed, it stays together for a long time.

Feeding: Feed the cichlids frozen foods that have been thawed for one to two days: smelts, large insects, and shrimp (freezer compartment). Characins, catfish, and oscars need fairly large quantities of green foods in addition, such as pieces of zucchini, lettuce leaves, etc. Don't use pellet foods or food mixes based on the flesh of warm-blooded animals—they will cause digestive problems.

A splendid spiny pleco (*Pseudacanthicus leopardus*).

Tank for Small Fish

Biotope: The aquarium should portray a quiet, sunny area of a weed-filled stream in Southeast Asia.

Population: A school of dwarf rasboras (genus *Boraras*), a group of a small *Badis* species, a pair of small gouramis, 10 dwarf shrimp.

Tank: 32 × 14 × 16 in (80 × 35 × 40 cm).

Water: Water type 2, peat filtration (see page 24).

Temperature: 79°F (26°C).

Lighting: One daylight fluorescent lamp and one Grolux (plant-growth) fluorescent lamp.

Mosquito rasboras are seen to advantage only in a school.

Dario cf. Dario accepts only live foods.

Honey gouramis build foam nests at the water surface.

Water movement: None.
Décor/Plantings: Place two small Java moss-covered roots so that they divide the bottom surface into three areas and rise up toward the tank background. The background should be densely planted with stem plants of various species. Liverwort (*Riccia*), used as a floating plant, will shade the tank in parts and provide a substrate for the gouramis' nest-building. Along the sides and in the middle, plant a *Cryptocoryne* that will stay small. In the middle tank region, place a solitary *Barclaya*.
Feeding: Twice a day, live *Artemia* nauplii, *Cyclops*, water fleas, small mosquito larvae (all live), small food flakes. Be sure not to overfeed the fish by putting too much food in the tank.

Rapids Tank

A pair of slender humpheads, the male above.

Biotope: The tank simulates a rock channel with strong water current in the rapids of the Lower Congo.

Population: Rapids cichlids form territories with Congo cichlids on the bottom, while a group of Congo tetras enlivens the open water column. Slender *Synodontis brichardi* (possible as algae eaters: *Ancistrus*).

Tank: 60 × 20 × 20 in (150 × 50 × 50 cm).

Water: Water type 3 (see page 24).

Temperature: 77°F (25°C).

Lighting: Two daylight fluorescent lamps and one Grolux (plant-growth) lamp.

TIP

Rapids
The Congo River widens as it approaches a rocky region to form the lakelike Pool Malebo. At the narrow outlet of this pool, the water works its way through rocky rapids to the Atlantic. The rapids provide a home to many fish that are found only in this location, because they have adapted to the extreme biotope of the Congo rapids.

Water movement: Create water movement primarily in the front third of the tank, with a strong centrifugal (rotary) pump that has its outlet on one side of the tank, while its intake is shifted to the other side by means of a PVC pipe.

Décor/Plantings: In the rear two-thirds, on a .4-in (1-cm) thick Styrofoam slab, layer flat stones (stone slabs) to a level about one-third the tank height. Pile them so as to create a great many hiding places of various sizes. On the slabs, place two elongated roots that

Various Congo tetras are suitable for a rapids tank.

are overgrown with Congo fern and extend in places up to the water surface.

Feeding: Once a day, dry foods (tablets, flakes) containing *Spirulina* algae. Once a day, fine live or frozen foods (*Artemia, Cyclops,* black or white mosquito larvae). Feed shrimp food specially developed for shrimp. Be sure not to overfeed the fish by putting too much food in the tank.

Brichard's Synodontis (*Synodontis brichardi*).

General Index

Page numbers in **boldface** refer to photos.

Index of Latin Fish Names

Page numbers in **boldface** refer to photos.

Cover photo: Firemouth cichlid **Back cover:** Cuckoo catfish (top); dwarf gourami (center); Louisiana dwarf crayfish (bottom).

The Photographers
Abel; Anders; blickwinkel (Zurlo); Bork; Büscher; Eigelshofen; Evers; Hartl; Hecker (Sauer); Hellner; Hippocampus Bildarchiv; Kahl; Kasselmann; Kilian; Linke; Lucas; Minde; Nieuwenhuizen; Peither; Reinhard; Schliewen; Schmida; Schraml; Spreinat; Staeck; Weidner; Werner; Wildekamp; Zurlo.

Conversion Chart

1 inch = 2.5 centimeters   1 gallon = 4 liters   °C = 5/9 (°F − 32)
